A Sequel to It's Supposed to Kill You

Now I'm ALIVE!

DOROTHY J. LEE

Print information available on the last page.

ISBN: 978-1-4907-8951-4 (sc)
ISBN: 978-1-4907-8956-9 (e)

Trafford rev. 07/06/2018

 www.trafford.com
North America & international
toll-free: 1 888 232 4444 (USA & Canada)
fax: 812 355 4082

Those who sow in tears shall reap with joyful shouting - Psalm 126:5

Contents

New books will emerge that will help us apply —in our culture.

<u>Veronika West</u>

I saw the Whirlwind of the Fear of the Lord coming swiftly and suddenly to tear down the idols of celebrity preachers and prophets, the idols of worship and entertainment and the idols of personal prosperity in His Church

FOREWORD

I met my spiritual mother, apostle Dorothy Lee, 12 years ago.

It is not difficult for me to call her Mom because she is a true nourisher. One of the things I learned about Mom is she is what she says she is.

You can see the fruit of who she claims to be. You can tell she is from God. Another thing I learned from her is you can fake friendship, but you can't fake covenant. She's turned out to be the epitome of what covenant is and what it means to join the community of Christ.

Through her steadfastness, I've learned to become a son with God's help - who taught me not to worry about if she was a mother or not. He told me to concentrate on being a son. As a result, I've learned more from watching her life than what came from her mouth.

Anything you would read in this book should automatically come alive to you, because there is no doubt that the author has lived it.

Jacques C. Cook, Original

Patrick Deaton:

"Dorothy Lee is truly a captivating woman of God with an irreplaceable role in His Kingdom. Her personal story of the heart of a woman pushed aside, wounded, and buried for many years in an abusive marriage is life changing. We believe her choice to stay obedient and submitted (underneath and dependent) first to the word, and then to her husband, is the source of her wisdom, stature, and favor with God. Spend a moment in her presence you will experience the intimate, living knowledge of God that dwells in the core of her being."

She willingly shares her secret life, open with God to all who come to her with open hearts. Her life and her words of wisdom will encourage you to enter the secret place of His Presence, sit before him, remove every façade and mask of pretense, and reveal to Him the innermost secrets of your heart.

It is a journey of Honesty worth taking as she leads you in the truths that led to her liberation from living as a servant and entering into the indescribable joy of living as a daughter of God."

Pastor Robert Daniels, City of the Lord Zion, Oakland, CA

"Dorothy Lee has been a good friend for over 20 years. I've known Dorothy to be a true worshiper and lover of God. A compassionate apostle of

Christ, who walks in holiness, faithfulness and integrity. Dorothy's sensitive, yet hard-hitting message challenges the saints of God to walk in maturity."

Harrison Lee:

"Dorothy Lee is someone I've known my entire life. As a child I knew her to be the uncompromisingly dutiful daughter to a man whose power and intelligence made him the center of our family and the community as well. That man was my grandfather and someone I revere to this day. Dorothy was the perfect caregiver as well when this man's world was shaken by his singular divorce. She was angelic in a time of secular upheaval, and that aura still emanates. That aura continued as she married and had three sons. It all seemed so normal and perfect. What I did not see was her devotions to faith in an aggressively secular life, one shrouded in the benefits of material wealth in the name of medicine. Dorothy is very traditional, as her father's favorite, and later lived as a dutiful, humble wife. This is something I had known all my life in my family. But God had other plans and challenges. Dorothy was pushed into acting and making decisions in the blink of an eye as her husband's health failed. Dorothy as God's handmaiden, let God be seen as her inspiration. This book and her life are the result." *(I mean it. By writing you put yourself in a very vulnerable place. You have to believe that truth as you've found it, is infectious, and words are its medium. It also means that you as its shield bearer are a target and a representative. You have to be strong.)*

NOW I'M ALIVE!

Introduction

It is a faithful saying: For if we be dead with him, we shall also live with him:
If we suffer, we shall also reign with him: if we deny him, he also will deny us. (2 Timothy 2:11-12, KJV)

With many tears and much praise, through my wilderness journey since 1969, I learned through obeying the Lord that I must be a Doer of the Word, to sow what I wanted to reap, and to trust Him for the results. I had no idea that those "seeds" I sowed would produce Christ in me, I just wanted to please God. The Bible tells us that Jesus is the Word made flesh, and that we must be Doers of the Word so that we won't be deceived, but it isn't that clear that **living/practicing/doing His Word in our lives is what "kills" us and Reproduces Him in us.**

I do not pretend or claim that I know the fullness of what this new life Is.. **far** from it…but by the faith of the Son of God, and because He has said it is **now my season** I am sharing with you the new Resurrection life the Lord has produced in me as I was willing to walk in His ways of the Cross.

There are other ministers that have experienced much more of the manifestation of power and the gifts of the spirit, but God chose me **to give His Life and Love to the Body**, and the Lord has repeatedly emphasized that my part is significant and needed, and will include all the other giftings and power also. He said that because I have given myself to Him without limit, that He would give me His Spirit without Measure. I do not doubt God. His ways are perfect. He does all things in Love, in Wisdom, in Power and in His Faithfulness, and He has anointed me to do his will in my life.

Chapter 1

Prophetic Words Given To Me

"MEN of wealth will come and seek your favor because you have Words of Life that change hearts; you cut through man's teachings and thinking and give the real Peace; They'll seek your favor, your blessing, your teaching;"

"HIS WORDS through you will drip with anointing, increase, and the breaker anointing and impartation of victory to see the Church AWAKENED WITH FIRE to the greater revelation of LIBERTY & VICTORY."

"WRITE with the pen of transparency of heart and revelation. The words will seem at first like innocent snowflakes falling. Then without warning, these words will gather momentum, causing spiritual blizzard conditions"

I have always been so hungry for God that I didn't mind that the years kept passing by without seeing much of the fulfillment of the hundreds of prophetic words I had received. I always turned to the Word and encouraged myself at how long others had to wait, and determined that I would stay strong in my faith like Caleb. But I have to admit I never imagined that the Lord would have me wait for over 48 years before calling me forth at this age of 82. So whatever the Lord accomplishes through my life, there will be no question that He is the One who accomplished it, because He has certainly taken the time to bring me to the end of myself!

I was particularly encouraged by these recent Prophetic words as they are both a confirmation and a continuing inspiration to me.

Restoring The Years

One of the promises of God that has been at the forefront in my life is Joel 2:25 (KJV)

> *And I will restore to you the years that the locust hath eaten, the cankerworm, and the caterpillar, and the palmerworm, my great army which I sent among you*
> *You shall eat in plenty and be satisfied, And praise the name of the Lord your God, Who has dealt wondrously with you; And My people shall never be put to shame.*

"You're About To Receive a God-Makeover!" by Lonnie Mackley 3/3/18

There are some of you who have been in the Christian Wilderness for many years now that are in desperate need of major restoration with your health and appearance, and God wants you to know today that He has already planned to give you a "God make-over" soon where He will miraculously restore and rejuvenate you in every way, rather than you spending thousands of dollars to try to put yourself back together again before this last harvest.

The Lord planned all of this from the beginning even before you went into your wilderness because He wants to get all the glory for restoring you, and He wants you to be a walking, talking billboard of His mighty miracles where He can send you out to help others to receive a "God make-over" from Him and believe that He's real and get saved.

You may be wondering what kinds of things that God is going to do to restore you, and from what I have seen it will be anything and everything you need in order to be fully ready for this harvest and the tribulation that will follow.

This means, weight loss, hair growth, new teeth or gold teeth, healing of your eyesight where you won't need glasses or contacts, becoming taller, healing of everything that has been wrong with your body no matter what it is even down to the smallest things, and even actual rejuvenation where your age is reversed just like Caleb in the bible was in a much younger body at the age of 85! Once this begins it will have a domino effect on your faith and you will go to bed one way, and wake up seeing new changes from the Holy Spirit overnight while you have slept.

What you are going to experience is not a hard thing for God and He wants to show off to the world through what He does for and through you, as well as vindicate you before some of the people that thought you were just a crazy loser all of these years for trusting God and living the way you have. This is a day of excitement and jubilee, and it gives God great joy to do these things for His beloved precious children that have been faithful to Him through their long wilderness ordeal. So get excited, and no matter what old pain you may be feeling today or what new wrinkle you saw in the mirror this morning rejoice that even your old wrinkles will start going away without any miracle cream, but with an actual miracle! God loves you so much, so take hope today and be ready for a God-makeover!'"// end -

Many years ago the Lord actually gave me a picture of a "makeover" of a disciple who came to my house and had a huge breakthrough. In the vision He allowed me to see her face close up. She had been living with environmental allergies which affected her health and appearance, but now she had glowing skin, luxurious hair, including her eyebrows and lashes, - and even the shape of her face was changed! — and then I saw her face actually start to change shape in the natural that very week at the next prayer meeting.

> *"Now then, just as the LORD promised, he has kept me alive for forty-five years since the time he said this to Moses, while Israel moved about in the desert. So here I am today, eighty-five years old! I am still as strong today as the day Moses sent me out; I'm just as vigorous to go out to battle now as I was then."* (JOS 14:10)

> *The righteous **will** flourish like a palm tree,*
> ***they will** grow like a cedar of Lebanon; planted in the house of the Lord,*
> ***they will** flourish in the courts of our God.*
> ***They will** still **bear fruit** in **old age,***
> ***they will** stay fresh and green* (Psalm 92:12-14)

Now that I'm in my 80's I am experiencing life more abundantly exactly as the Lord promises in His Word - that our latter years would be greater than the former and that we elders would continue to bear fruit in our old age, and that He would renew and restore to us all that has been lost or stolen - including our youth.

God has flooded my heart with peace and His joy which is my strength. I am feasting at His banqueting table continually. He has set a table before me in the presence of my enemies. He has caused me to Overcome so that I am inheriting ALL things, He is making me a pillar, I'm seated on His throne with Him in His authority and I am now eating of the Tree of Life which is in the Paradise of God. His Word is being fulfilled in my life as He is faithful to all those who trust and obey Him. There is an expected end! He cannot lie or fail or deny His Word. --I don't know what my end will look like exactly, but I know I will experience His fullness for me and in me, and I want it! And I want to be able to pour into others as long as He keeps me alive. He said the last enemy we will overcome is Death - so I am in anticipation to see what that looks like.

I was told that I used to have to fight to overcome, but now that I'm older, others are called to be praying and fighting for me so that I can rest and worship which is my assignment now. God is still moving through me but in a different way. He is still building His house and I am going to keep trusting Him and following Him into the fullness of my inheritance and destiny and His purposes. I'm going to keep believing His Word and not lean to my own understanding so that I don't hinder God's will. I will not limit God in what He desires to do in my life so that I can be an example and demonstration of His Kingdom in me for His glory and honor.

I remember how it felt to begin sowing the Word into my life and then practicing being a doer, but now in these latter days of my life, <u>I am tasting and seeing more of the harvest and it is grand!</u>

The fruit of the Spirit that is manifesting now is nothing like the seed. We cannot imagine how sowing the seed of His Word into our lives will produce His Kingdom in us. We read that Christ is in us and yet He is to be formed in us, and we must experience this new life. To experience it is very different - beyond our imagination. <u>Being faithful in all those "little" things has</u> <u>truly produced the "much increase"</u> promised to us.

In a prophetic word entitled "**<u>Seniors On The Frontlines</u>" <u>by</u>** Paulette Reed, we are reminded of how God used Abraham and Sarah in their advanced years, even though they too, like us present day seniors, thought they were too old to give birth to a dream. Of course we know that they did give birth to their dreams, and the Lord is telling us to believe also that we will be used in our senior years to birth dreams and that we are not too old.

If we will just truly believe, the Lord is telling us that we too will experience restoration, revival and reformation bursting forth, and He is calling us, the Seniors, to the front lines at this time!.

He is about to visit us and fill us with His strength, mercy, power, and faithfulness. Angels will be assisting us at conception, labor, and delivery of God's promises, and businesses, books, ministries, and more will be birthed supernaturally with ease.

For He has tried and tested us. We have been disciplined, chastened and brought through the fire as pure gold; and Gold is the latter glory; and this glory is greater than the former.

Abraham and Sarah's baby was named Isaac which we know means "laughter", and as Sarah laughed, we too will laugh and carry a joy unspeakable for the world to see. The Lord is about to visit those of us seniors who believe and He will bless us so that we can be a blessing even to nations.

In another word, <u>**"Seniors Redefined"**</u> Patricia King was shown a company of radical Believers in their 60's, 70's, 80's and beyond -that will arise and experience personal revival that will reignite their passion and purpose. These seniors are full of wisdom, zeal and they carry dreams yet to be fulfilled.

She saw them <u>walking with the younger generations and empowering them with encouragement, and they in return will</u> be honored and respected by the younger generation.

These seniors will be a **<u>sought after</u>** <u>generation,</u> and many will rise into places of **predominance** and **leadership in their fields of service**. They will **produce more fruit** with **less effort** than they put forth in their former years.

<u>**Financial increase**</u> will come to them and **<u>Favor will rest</u>** upon them. A wave of <u>**healing, health, and rejuvenation in body, soul, and spirit**</u> will visit them. They will be <u>**filled with overflowing joy**</u>! and will <u>**step**</u>

<u>into supernatural realms of glory and power</u> in ways that the world will have no doubt that God is in the midst of them.

These seniors will <u>manifest strength, vision and longevity (there will be many who will live past "one hundred years" of age enjoying active and productive lives.) - along with their fruitfulness and prosperity,</u> more than any generation of seniors since the resurrection of Jesus Christ. They will <u>finish strong.</u>

<u>"55s and Over, Thrive and Shine!"</u> by Lana Vawser

The Lord told Lana that the "55s and over are a key!" What the over 50s CARRY is a KEY to UNLOCK more of what God is desiring to manifest in the Church and into the nations. There is going to be a great UNLOCKING that will take place and it will be through those 55 and older!

"Heavenly wisdom will be unlocked and restored in many ways in the Body of Christ through these 55 and over."

I saw treasure chests of heavenly wisdom and revelation stored within many of these 55s and over but I saw JESUS HIMSELF placing His hand of release and activation upon these treasure chests that were deep within their hearts. SUDDENLY, wisdom and revelation were flowing out like tidal waves into the Body of Christ. **The wisdom and revelation brought an even greater unlocking, activation and impartation in the Body of Christ.**

Many over 55 who have passionately sought after wisdom, chased after it, positioned themselves for it, and it has cost them a lot, but they had great revelation that *wisdom is the most valuable commodity. (see* **Proverbs 4:7**)

It's time for these 55s and over to arise in greater ways, because a significant shifting season is upon them.

"IT'S TIME TO THRIVE AND SHINE!"

In accordance with these prophetic words, in this second book I am writing, I am sharing the new life God formed and produced in me through His process of my dying, and the wonderful Harvest I am enjoying, and of course with MUCH more than I know - yet to come.

I had always heard that the hardest part is the "waiting" and although I never dreamed I would be waiting over 48 years, it's still more than worth it and I know God's timing is perfect. I can see so much of what He has built into my life and I know that every bit will be needed and nothing wasted. I know that I will have no regrets because I wouldn't want to step out into ministry without being fully prepared, and I know only God knows what preparation is needed.

I recently heard a video about some of the great healing evangelists and about all the signs and wonders that surrounded them. But the Lord said He would **"never again pour out such power**

on a man without Holiness" because of all the corruption that evolved. And I for one totally agree - I wouldn't want to be in a place of great signs and wonders without having been sanctified by the Spirit, because I never want to end up taking His glory to myself and being ashamed before God.

My union with Him is the most important thing to me - absolutely, without question. I want Him to take as long as I need it to be faithful to Him in all I do. He's had to deliver me from so much and I trust Him totally. In fact, "trust" is one of the main things He has been building in me. It makes me so happy that He took me through the process that has caused me to be weak in myself and to really need to lean on my Beloved, since that's what He knows will keep us close to Him and safe from corrupting the precious gifts He gives us.

> *The glory which You have given Me I have given to them, that they may be one, just as We are one;* (John 17:22, NASB)

The process of dying to ourself Is painful beyond imagination; however the resurrection life we are given out of that death is **more** than Beyond imagination. It is an on-going, increasingly glorious experience, — all at the same time and a continual discovery all at the same time. We have never known this existence before; - it is to live a supernatural life naturally. Having a new life, is just that. It's not something you have to think about doing, it just IS!....you just become!

"A Treasure Beyond Measure!
by **Johannes VD Hoven**

Finding someone who has journeyed with the Lord in a lifetime of surrender and in whom the Stature of Christ has grown to maturity - Is finding a gem!

A pearl of great price that should be embraced as being valuable beyond measure.

For such a one becomes a well-spring of Living Water that will nourish every life connected to themand will cause everything they touch to explode with new Life!

The journey is not easy, nor is it instant. It is a lifelong timeous process of dying to Live.

Therefore it is true that those in whom the Lord is formed are rare -

Just as there are many oysters, among which one oyster may be found among the many, that contains a pearl of great price.

When you find them. TREASURE Christ in them! Yes, the Treasure is Christ who is formed in us.

CROSSING OVER:

> *Faithful is the [a]saying: For if we died with him, we shall also live with him: if we endure, we shall also reign with him: if we shall deny him, he also will deny us: 13 if we are faithless, he abideth faithful; for he cannot deny himself.* (2 Timothy 2:11-13, ASV)

By **Glenn Jackson** (**Excerpt**): "Why do you think we've been suffering such a long painful travail bride of Jesus Christ? God the Father spoke audibly through Isaiah 66 to me about our imminent Spiritual catching up that shall be the greatest KINGDOM OF GOD CORPORATE SHIFT in the entire history of the church.

He declared, "<u>those who have submitted themselves to the road of the cross through self-denial are the ones that shall be raised up by God to operate as 1 nation under God.</u>"

By **Lonnie Mackley** Feb. 2018 "My dear one, your day to rise has come and now <u>I will take you from the small world you have</u> <u>been used to, and place you into a large world</u> that is greatly in need of My help. I will fulfill all of the words I have spoken to you and none of them will go unfulfilled. You will indeed see and believe that I am the same God in the end that called you from the beginning so long ago, and <u>now you will begin to experience</u>

the opposite of many of the things you have been used to all of your life. Now comes the great turnaround!"

In my first book "It's Supposed to Kill You" I shared many of the Ways of God that He taught me to walk in. And now that I have been walking in His Ways for over 4 decades, I can confidently say His Ways work! His Word is True! He really did it all for us - He saved us, sanctified us, washed us, delivered us, healed us and gave us His Spirit to dwell in us, to teach us, to help us, to lead us, to reveal mysteries and to quicken us and anoint us — but it was all accessed by being teachable and obedient to His Word and His Ways. The path of the just is as a shining light that gets brighter and brighter. We do go from strength to strength and glory to glory as we become DOERS of the WORD and not hearers only.

I not only learned the ways of God in order to go through the Dying process, but I have also learned that "Dying to our Self" is not an end, but it is making a way and it is preparing us for the New Resurrection Life we will have in Christ.

Christians who have not taken up their cross unto the death of their flesh, often challenge me that this narrow path is not for everyone, but the Lord Himself taught me these things and I have lived them and experienced the process and the outcome personally. And I know that we cannot fully experience our salvation and see the total fulfillment of our destiny without going through the process of dying and being raised to the new life in His image by being Doers of His Word and not hearers only. We should believe God that He has given each of us only a part, so we still need each other's parts to be complete, EVEN MY PART, but it is still our choice.

I don't know where the end of the process of dying is, but I do know by what He has taught me and worked into me, that He is making me an Overcomer in every challenge of my life, to walk in His commandments victoriously instead of by my own feelings or opinions, so that I am growing more and more in the image of Christ and the Fruit of the Spirit has become my daily delight, and the Word says I will inherit all things. And it means I live in intimacy with the Lord so I have the grace to be continually teachable and to have faith in Him, as I've learned that His ways are perfect, that He will remain faithful to perfect that which concerns me and that everything I've been through will work together for my good.

> *but as it is written, [a]Things which eye saw not, and ear heard not, And which entered not into the heart of man, Whatsoever things God prepared for them that love him.* (1 Corinthians 2:9, American Standard Version ASV)

In God's wisdom He has waited to see if his people would take heed to His warnings to be doers of his word and not hearers only, to keep his Commandments and obey his will. (read 1 Corinthians 10 and Psalms 78)

> *To the pure you show yourself pure, but to the wicked you show yourself hostile.* (Psa 18:26, NLT).

Those who have trusted and obeyed the Lord and His word, will experience this new life, but those who do not obey His Word will never experience what the Lord has prepared for them because they will follow the idols of their own hearts and be deceived into thinking they hear from God. (see Ezekiel 14:3-4 and James 3: 13- 17) When we don't become Doers of His Word and learn to Love, we will be blind, and when a person is blind, he cannot see. But if anyone would take heed to God's word, he will see where the fruit of his life doesn't line up with the fruit of His Spirit, where he is not growing into His image and by His grace he could repent instead of being offended by those who live and speak the truth in love.

> *These things have I spoken unto you, that ye should not be caused to stumble. They shall put you out of the synagogues: yea, the hour cometh, that whosoever killeth you shall think*

*that he offereth service unto God. And
these things will they do, because they
have not known the Father, nor me.*
(John 16:1-3, ASV)

*But be ye doers of the word, and
not hearers only, deluding your own
selves.* (James 1:22, ASV)

As the Lord told me, every commandment
was designed to kill a part of our flesh. Therefore
in any area where we are not obeying Him and
His commandments (as He leads by His peace)
we will not even see the salvation God has given
us. We will not even realize what we have missed
like the pharisees. The pride, the rebellion, the
stubbornness of our flesh, will deceive us.

The word says the truth will set us free, so if we
do not even know the truth we certainly will not
experience the freedom God has provided for us. We
will not even know it Is available because we'll be so
busy judging/blaming others. (see 1John 2:11)

But to <u>those who OBEY all things are made
known</u>. God cannot be mocked. We will reap what
we have sown whether we like it or not. We can
choose what and when we sow to some extent, but
we have little control over what we will reap. Our
harvest is determined by what we have sown, unless
God mercifully intervenes.

I have learned that God is exact in what He
says, in what He requires, and what He promises.

We just need to trust and obey. We cannot save ourselves. We cannot earn our salvation. Our righteousness is as filthy rags. He says His ways are above our ways and that there's a way that seems right but that way leads to death. And since broad is the way to destruction, we know that most Christians live by what seems right to them instead of obeying His Word and choosing the narrow path of the Cross that leads to life.

Chapter 2

The Word/His Commandments

We will never understand the significance of His Word in our lives unless we apply it and start to live it. If we study His Word to just gain knowledge about Jesus, to prepare for a sermon or class, or to make ourselves look good, we will never experience the marvel of our salvation. It is Idolatry. - (Read Rom 2:17)

If we study the word just to find out how to gain power, or to see how to perform miracles, we're just giving ourselves to Him to get what we want, and we are actually Prostituting ourselves. But the Lord said "Go and learn what that means." How many have taken this step to go and learn from the Spirit what the Word should mean to us personally as we are studying it? We can fool ourselves and others, but we can never fool God. Only the pure in heart will see God, but our hearts are wickedly deceitful and who can know it?, It takes a hunger and a consecration to get beyond the surface of the Word in order to find life. and be filled with it.

So what does walking on the narrow path produce in our life?

<u>The Word</u> becomes our life - we must learn to trust the Word as we trust God since they are ONE. Jesus is the Word made flesh and that's what He wants to accomplish in our lives. That is why He allows us to go through so many trials - so we can practice/learn to LIVE by His Word (Matthew 4:4) - the truth must be so real to us that we totally depend on it. We have peace in our trials, or at least we fight to be at peace so we can be led by Him. (see Col 3:15)

We must put our entire weight on the promises/ Word of God, until there is no more fear, frustration, anger, anxiety, bitterness, or striving in our life. We will have perfect REST because we have (progressively) learned how faithful He is (as we have obeyed and believed) and know what it is to be ONE with Him.

This process takes us from obedience to believe, to actually believing, which is FAITH which works by LOVE (God's love), which causes us to Trust Him, which will lead us into His REST. This is a faith that God produces and forms in us through all the trials and testings as we keep believing His Word. This is how the Word becomes Flesh in US! Being Born Again is not just being saved but it's coming to the place in our salvation of having His character and image. There must be a supernatural quickening of the Word in our lives where we don't just "know and do" but we "become and are".

> *By this we come to know (recognize and understand) that we love the children of God: <u>when we love</u> <u>God and obey His commands (orders, charges)</u> [when we keep His ordinances and are mindful of His precepts and His teaching].*
> *For the [true] love of God is this: that we do His commands [keep His ordinances and are mindful of His precepts and teaching]. And these orders of His are not irksome (burdensome, oppressive, or grievous). For <u>whatever is born of God</u> is victorious over the world; and this is the the victory that conquers the world, even <u>our faith.</u> (emphasis mine)* (1John 5:2-4, AMPC)

> *You have been born anew, not of perishable but of imperishable seed, through the living and enduring word of God.* (1 Peter 1:23, NRSVA)

> *But if you call yourself a Jew and rely on the law and boast in God and know his will and approve what is excellent, because you are instructed from the law; and if you are sure that you yourself are a guide to the blind,*

a light to those who are in darkness, an instructor of the foolish, a teacher of children, having in the law the embodiment of knowledge and truth— you then who teach others, do you not teach yourself? (Romans 2:17-29, ESV)

read (John 17:17; 1 Timothy 4:5; Revelation 1:2; Colossians 1:25).

For the word of God is living, and active, and sharper than any two-edged sword, and piercing even to the dividing of soul and spirit, of both joints and marrow, and quick to discern the thoughts and intents of the heart. Jesus showed a link between the written Word of God and Himself, in that He is the subject of the written Word: (Hebrews 4:12, American Standard Version ASV)

[a]Ye search the scriptures, because ye think that in them ye have eternal life; and these are they which bear witness of me; (John 5:39, American Standard Version ASV)

One prophet shared a word about "Truth bombs" falling, and the false being blown away by prophets with an unction from the Holy Spirit, who were boldly proclaiming truth for the hour at hand.

In a vision she saw soldiers who were living epistles; the voices of Truth in the earth. They stood on the Word and allowed it to have full reign in their lives.

She shared that God is sending a fresh wind of His Spirit that will bring forth a boldness to the prophets to speak the Truth, and it will also bring a separation of the true from the false; shackles will break, and the light of Truth will pierce into the heart, allowing the penetration of God's love into the deepest wounds of the soul. There will be a great revealing of truth that will expose lies, an un-covering of ancient wells and an excavation of hidden treasures, for the release of supplies for His army rising.

The Word of God is alive it sustains man (Luke 4:4), it brings faith (Romans 10:17), it has freedom to accomplish God's will (2 Timothy 2:9), it gives spiritual birth (1 Peter 1:23), and it abides within believers (1 John 2:14).

Commentator Matthew Henry wrote of the Bible that it "convinces powerfully, converts powerfully, and comforts powerfully. It makes a soul that has long been proud, to be humble; and a perverse spirit, to be meek and obedient. Sinful habits are being separated and cut off by this sword. It will discover to men their thoughts and purposes, the vileness of many, the bad principles they are moved by, the sinful ends they act to" (*Concise Commentary on the Whole Bible*, <u>Hebrews 4:11–16</u>).

The living Word is active in the lives of those who receive it. According to the psalmist, the person who meditates on and delights in the Word will be "like a tree planted by streams of water, which yields its fruit in season and whose leaf does not wither" (<u>Psalm 1:2–3</u>). The Scriptures today are often downplayed in favor of manmade philosophies, personal experiences, or a "new" word from God. But the Bible cannot be ignored as if it were dead or obsolete. The Word of God is still powerful and very much alive. "We also have the prophetic message as something completely reliable, and you will do well to pay attention to it, as to a light shining in a dark place, until the day dawns and the morning star rises in your hearts" (<u>2 Peter 1:19</u>).

> *And a highway shall be there, and a way, and it shall be called The way of holiness; the unclean shall not pass over it; but it shall be for the redeemed: the wayfaring men, yea fools, shall not err therein. No lion shall be there, nor shall any ravenous beast go up thereon; they shall not be found there; but the redeemed shall walk there: and the ransomed of Jehovah shall return, and come with*

singing unto Zion; and everlasting joy shall be upon their heads: they shall obtain gladness and joy, and sorrow and sighing shall flee away. (Isaiah 35:8-10, American Standard Version ASV)

It's time to believe God's Word that we will be known by our FRUIT - not our GIFTS - when we become a mature Body. (see Matt 7:16-20) as we die, He lives His life through us and in His perfection He is the one who perfectly fulfills all His promises. He perfects that which concerns us by taking over and living through us.

The beautiful thing about **God's commands** is that yes, they're set up to give us exactly what we need to die to ourselves, but then they also perfectly set us up for our prosperity and blessings. As we plant the seed of His word in us through obedience, and then water it with our faith and stay close to the presence of God, that seed will absolutely produce after it's kind! It will look like Jesus! We'll be one of His "brethren" - holy like Him.

As we walk (obey) daily with Jesus, the more He inhabits us and the more we are being prepared to become the expression of His very being.(see John 14:2) We are becoming the likeness of His death and so we will walk in the likeness of His resurrection - (see Romans 6:4.)

So many of God's people fear to take up their crosses and lose their life, but it's time to realize and wake up to the truth that "losing our life" in God's way is the only way to possess the Kingdom, and in reality, our "loss" is no loss at all because He says we will actually Save it - so we will experience ONLY GAIN and ABUNDANT LIFE in the end.. Our flesh does not die without a fight, but if we yield, once we taste the new life, we will rejoice.

Sadhu Selvaraj prophesied recently that this is the year (2018) to prepare for God's glory - 7 fold. He said it's right at the door, so we must be ready. - Marching orders will be given and we must be prepared to go then. There will be no time to wait."

So this is where we are now. We must stop being double minded and decide if we want to be conformed to the Lord's image by dying to ourselves or not. **Time for making choices and preparing ourselves is NOW.** Our eternal destiny rests on the choice we make in this hour. It is not possible for us to change ourselves to become like Christ - only by letting Him take you through your fiery trials will it happen. Be not deceived - don't fool yourself, there's no other way - gold must be refined by fire. You must be willing to pay the price, but God's grace is sufficient for you. He will work it in you to will and do His will, but we must choose and not waiver because the Word says he that waivers will not receive anything.

I used to waiver all over the place. I didn't like the thought of choosing to suffer and I was fearful of what I would have to go through, but as I kept calling on the Lord to help me overcome my fear, I found that His grace was carrying me through my trials and it was not as difficult as I thought. The pain was real, but there was always a breakthrough and a new level of His presence and His peace and love. And as I obeyed to trust Him, there was always new grace and strength to continue on.

We must realize it is utterly foolish to complain about giving up our filthy rags because He will replace them with royal priestly garments. Any sacrifice we make for the Lord always brings us a reward from Him even though it makes no sense. How is it that when we repent for sin of which we are guilty - we get rewarded? It's no wonder it is said you can't out give God, because it's so true!

The Word says we have not because we don't ask, or we ask and don't receive because we ask amiss. We must choose and <u>ask</u> <u>for HIS WILL</u> in our life. It's our choice, but when we ask for what is our own will, many times He won't answer us because He knows if we are asking for what will be harmful for us or not His best for us... but if we persist, He may relent and give us our "quail". I have learned to seek Him for His will in all things. I don't want anything outside of His will for my life. I don't want second best - I don't want "quail", I want His perfect will - I want ALL of me to be of HIM and only Him.

When we will obey the Lord at all times, we are **totally safe from all the weapons formed against us - even unknown ones.** Salvation is sure when we walk uprightly and our joy will be everlasting in

Him - not in things. <u>We will see all His promises fulfilled</u> because we've walked in obedience so that the blessings and prosperity He bestows on us will not destroy us - lusts and greed will not overtake us and we will remain steadfast and faithful to the

Lord - which should be the most important thing to our hearts. He is more important to us than any things we will receive - but obeying the Lord will produce things in our lives that we've not seen nor heard of nor even have entered our imagination.

Our Father has longed to bless and prosper His children abundantly above all we know to ask or think but <u>He has to wait for our maturity so that we will not be destroyed and so we can be mature enough to value what He values</u>. Building our house on the sand is just selecting a piece of the word here and there as it suits us - instead of being a <u>Doer of the Word and standing on the Rock as it pleases Him!</u>

By Johannes VD Hoven: "INCREASE YOUR ANOINTING IN ME..." What had happened in the 15 years that I did not have any contact with her, that caused such a radical change? (When Johannes saw someone he hadn't seen for 15 years, he was amazed at the change in her)

"As I walked away from the conference room I sensed the Holy Spirit clearly ministering to my heart. He said, "T<u>hat is the fruit of a life that grows in My Presence. The fruit of allowing me to grow</u>

in her, as she grows in Me. It is the reward of a matured life in Me. No quick fixes. No shortcuts. It's My work in time, unhurried, in a yielded vessel, who is a lover of My Presence and My will".

"I prayed a prayer that day that changed my dreams and my perspective forever - I said - **"Lord THAT IS what I want! I do not want Your Power without Your Presence - I WANT YOU TO BE SEEN IN ME! I WANT YOU TO GROW IN ME! Let it be so in me, let Your Presence grow in me, mature in me, and as the years progress, let others see more of You in me!"** //end

"Many seek the Anointing, many are confused about how it comes, and how it increases. There are many beliefs and philosophies....The truth is that the Anointing grows in us, as we continue to grow into the Presence of God. It increases not in measure, but in Revelation - The more transparent we become, the more of our Heavenly Father becomes visible through us, and the greater of a blessing He becomes to others through us!

"PRAY - HEAVENLY FATHER INCREASE YOUR ANOINTING IN ME, BECOME MORE VISIBLE IN MY LIFE - THEN YIELD TO HIS PROCESS AND ALLOW HIM TO ANSWER THAT PRAYER!"// end

Chastisement and trials are a major part of the narrow path. It is written that if we are without chastisement we are not even his sons, but illegitimate children. (see Hebrews 12) So if you are a true son, you would welcome His chastisement. You would realize that it is good for God to deal with our sin nature and we would be grateful to be free from sin. You would want to be pleasing to your Father and to do his will. And when trials come you would be thankful that God is cleansing you, humbling you and making you acceptable to him. He says that we are to be holy as He is holy and we would want that. Gold must be refined in fire, clay must be molded and put in the furnace, grapes must be crushed to produce wine, oysters must suffer to produce pearls. Tears endure for the night but joy comes in the morning.

> For it is after we have suffered that we shall be made whole. (see 1Peter 5:10, Psalms 138:1-8)

> *But if you are without chastening, of which all have become partakers, then you are illegitimate and not sons: Now no chastening seems to be joyful for the present, but painful; nevertheless, afterward it yields the peaceable fruit of righteousness to those who have been trained by it.* (Heb 12:8;11)

Although Salvation is free, we must pay the price if we want to become pure gold, or finest wine or a vessel of honor.

"Behold, I send My messenger, And he will prepare the way before Me. And the Lord, whom you seek, Will suddenly come to His temple, Even the Messenger of the covenant, In whom you delight. Behold, He is coming," Says the Lord of hosts.

"But who can endure the day of His coming? And who can stand when He appears? For He is like a refiner's fireAnd like launderers' soap.

He will sit as a refiner and a purifier of silver; He will purify the sons of Levi, And purge them as gold and silver, That they may offer to the Lord An offering in righteousness.

"Then the offering of Judah and Jerusalem Will be pleasant to the Lord, As in the days of old, As in former years.

And I will come near you for judgment; I will be a swift witness Against sorcerers,, Against adulterers, Against perjurers, Against those who exploit wage earners and widows and orphans, And against those who turn away an alien—Because they do not fear Me," Says the Lord of hosts.
(Malachi 3:1-5)

Chapter 3

LOVE AND LIFE: 1 John

For several decades the Lord has told me to read the Prophets daily and it has been such a blessing. At first the prophetic words spoke of things coming from far off, but the prophesied events came nearer and nearer, and then into view, to now where much is becoming a reality and I realize I'm now walking more and more in synch with the prophetic words.

In fact, one recent prophetic word startled me because everything in that word was describing what was going on in my life and ministry and the way I was moving with God in this present time.

And not only is my ministry in alignment with what the Lord is saying, but also I now presently enjoy the love, peace, and joy of the Kingdom, and I have the satisfaction of experiencing His love and nature flowing through me in my life every day. I am tasting and seeing that the Lord is good.

I no longer just believe the Word, but I am living it, because He is living His life through me now. His life in me is certainly not in fullness yet, but it is full in purity and surrender and submission of my heart to the Lord.

It may be difficult for some to hear new revelation when we're comfortable and confident with the old, but because the Lord birthed this in me, I cannot deny truth even though some may think it is heretical or at least prideful. But No, it's fact. The Lord has proven it to me by letting me progressively experience the victory and new life in Him as I obeyed. It's not me, because I have died (by the Lord's perfect trials), but now it's Christ living in me, and He is the perfect one. He can live His perfect life through us as long as we are willing to keep dying to our own will - or anything that resists Him from living through us. We must give Him our entire will, our trust, our obedience, our lives, and by dying to ourself, this is made possible.

As I was worshipping the Lord one time in the middle of the night, I was overwhelmed with tears of gratitude and joy at all He had done for me. In obeying His commandments, there is life, and there is the Kingdom and all the fruit of the Spirit - it's all made available to us through His Word and His Spirit - but it is not released to us unless we have chosen the pathway of Submission, Obedience and Trust. As the seeds have fallen into the ground (like Jesus) they bring forth the harvest. And when it's harvest time and the fruits are ripe, there is LIFE with so much sweetness and goodness and fullness of Him. We are meant to be satisfied and having pleasure in Him.

How is it possible that a mere human being can experience so much of the pleasure and significance of God in what has formerly been such an insignificant, painful and unrighteous life? How can this be conveyed to others who are walking in darkness and in chains and pain just like I was?

When you yourself have been rescued from your own pitiful pit, you want nothing more than to help others come out of their pits.

And the good news is the Lord showed me the way to get out through walking in His Ways, if we'll be teachable and obedient.

I was told recently that I know things that I don't know that I know. I thought that was kind of a riddle, but as I meditated on it, I could grasp somewhat that it was true. All I did was obey and trust God. He never explained the Why's or the What's to me. In fact He told me I had the blessing of those who believe though they do not see. So now at this juncture, I am experiencing this wonderful life, but I can't explain fully how He did it, nor am I yet aware of all He's done for me. - As I have stayed singled to Him, I keep discovering more and more of what He's done for me as I am continuing to walk with Him. The Word says the Kingdom comes without observation for the Kingdom of God is in us. (see Luke 17:20) This is so true.

The Word was made flesh and He dwelt among us,(see John 1:14) but it can be made flesh in us also and it can be seen that He dwells in us as He lives His life through us via our obedience. It's no wonder that the Lord tells us that we will know others by their fruit, because fruit is grown and we can't act like we have it.- and the fruit will be tasted and known by others.

Many Christians think they just have to go to church, do some Bible reading and praying and then go and DO Works for the Lord - but it'll never be authentic Christianity.

When wheat is ripe, it bows its head, but when tares are ripe, they stand fully, smugly, self-confidently upright. Authentic Christians will be bowed and humble like the Lord and all the fruit of the Spirit will be manifested in them.

We all have our own opinions about how to do things, and there are many teachings about how to live, but I have learned that the ONLY way we can live the life that's pleasing to the Lord and that will bear His fruit, is **a life of submission, obedience, faith, and trust that produces love, joy and peace.** And it is the pathway of Peace that gives us sure direction and leads to the new life promised to us in the 'Word".

> "**Love** brings joy, it brings peace. It brings sadness and grief.
> It brings hope, it brings pain, it drives people insane.

It brings smiles, it brings tears, it helps overcome fears. It's part of you, part of me, part of us, cause love is key." (author unknown)

"It is as My **children "abide" in My Love** that they shall **experience ALL that I have "ordained" for their life and ministry**. It is My desire to continually **"thrill" My children,** and do that **which exceeds abundantly** beyond all they can ask or think - at all times!" excerpt by Glenn Jackson

"God's greatest **desire is that His people would walk in love.**

Loving Him and then loving one another from the heart. We have to pursue Love but at the same time the Word says He has given us a spirit of love, power and a sound mind already."

It has amazed me how naturally we can learn to love if we obey His Word, because it's all Him (His Word). Receiving the depth of God's love for myself has enabled me to show love for others out of that same depth. I have found what it means that Love never fails. It doesn't always accomplish what we want, but it does always accomplish something good when we apply love in every encounter. It will work good either in us or the other person or both, but Love is not what man thinks it is.

One prophet spoke: '**Truth spoken in Love** - is the **distinguishing sound** in this hour - the HOUR of fulfillment of all things. It's the time for love to be manifested,** this is the day and the hour."

Prophets told me that I would be bringing Love and Life to the Body, that these were the gifts He had given me. I didn't understand what these gifts were at first, but with obedience, I have certainly learned. So now it's my great joy to share them with you.

1 Corinthians 13 says LOVE IS THE GREATEST GIFT

It's the gift that is the greatest blessing for both the bearer as well as the recipient. It ministers to the whole man and it increases with use. We cannot be God's voice or be His son or His Bride without love.

> *By this we know that we love the children of God, when we love God, and keep his commandments.* (1 John 5:2, KJV)

Practicing Love

It made me so happy to learn that just keeping His commandments is what Love is and we can choose to let it be expressed through us. Love may not have emotions at first, but it will as we persevere. Here's how we learn to love: (my version of 1 Corinthians 13)

We will choose and practice Patience and long suffering with everyone, including ourselves;

We will think and act in Kindness, especially with our mates and family - knowing it is imparting grace to them.

We won't envy others when they seemingly have something we wish we had because we've learned to be thankful and to know that God will fulfill His word to us also

We won't be boasting when it seems we're proven to be right; we will not have any pride in it, because we know God resists the proud and gives grace to the humble.

Our actions, heart condition and our words will not dishonor others because there will be nothing in us that is trying to exalt ourselves. We've learned to esteem others above ourselves.

We will not easily be angered because we are not willing to keep any record of wrongs...we've learned to cast down all criticism and judgments. We will not take delight in finding evil in others as if we're so discerning (pride), but we will rejoice with the Truth - which is how God sees things - that is, through His love. Therefore we will always protect others because we understand their situation, we will always trust God because we've come to know His faithfulness, we will always have hope because of how mighty God is, and we will always persevere because He has become our strength and we believe that His Love will never fail; **we rest** confidently in His promise of that."

I have never heard so many prophets speak on the same theme in all the years the Lord has had me reading the prophets - and that is **LOVE**. It's now that we will <u>see His love manifested and</u> <u>it will be</u> <u>Love that will distinguish between those who walk</u> <u>uprightly</u> <u>and those who are just pretending</u>.

<u>A gift that is exercised without love will not</u> <u>be life giving and</u> <u>the Word says it will profit us</u> <u>nothing. (1 Cor 13:3)</u> The Lord will <u>even tell us to</u> <u>depart from Him because He never knew us. (Matt</u> <u>7:21-23) We can't say we know God if we do not</u> <u>have love for we</u> <u>would be lying. (1John 2:4) The</u> <u>letter kills but the spirit gives life.</u> (2 Cor 3:6) This is true in our anointing, in our personal lives and in our words especially.

Bob Jones died and went to heaven (but came back) and he said the only thing he was asked when he got to the gate was "**Did** **you learn to love?**" We were born into this world as totally selfish beings which is why our flesh needs to die, but when we are born again, He wants us to be totally Unselfish beings - which equates to LOVE and which is only possible through Him.

You can't imagine how blessed I've been to read all the prophetic words about love, since that is one of my main gifts. From experience I can say I have mostly become love (as far as I can see in His Word) through His life in me.

In retrospect I realize that <u>the first steps into</u> <u>my new life</u> began in the early 2000's when the Lord told me "Now that you don't have anymore rebellion, now do not let your husband intimidate you anymore." This was an awkward thing for me to do after so many years of submission, but the Lord was beginning to teach me how to reign with Him. While you are still rebellious, your flesh wants to control others for your own selfish will, but when you die, He is in control and reigns through you to fully accomplish the Father's will.

As we continually obey God, it will work in us the power to love the Lord, then love ourselves, then our neighbor, and finally even our enemies; and as we exercise that love, it will work in us the power to love more and to experience more of Him.

The power to love - especially our enemies - is such a blessing because it burns out all the selfishness and accusations, and the resultant death working in us, and makes us more like Him. The Lord asks us to love our enemies that we may be perfect as He is. What God calls perfect is LOVE! So as we continually obey God and His commandments, His love fills us and flows through us to bring healing and freedom to ourselves and then to others. The Fear of the Lord is the beginning of Wisdom, and Love is the end result or Fulfillment of His wisdom.

God is love, so if we say we know Him or are serving Him and do not have continual love in our hearts for God and everyone else, we are being deceived, and unless we are pressing towards that goal, then we are just pretending to be Christians.

I have found that in practicing His Word to love, that I have been the first one to benefit. It leaves me feeling so good when I can return love to my enemies, when it's proven through trials that this love is true and not a performance. It is so great when my heart is always rightly positioned before God. That way, even <u>when</u> <u>false accusations are hurled against me, I don't have to think about</u> <u>what to do. I am prepared - always ready to love, to understand</u> <u>others, to bless them in return.</u>

Glenn Jackson shared: "The bottom line is, **if we are truly obeying the Lord and walking in His Ways, we will be walking in His commandments and they will produce LOVE in us.**"

The Word tells us that the **pure in heart shall see God.** This doesn't just mean seeing Him in intimacy and close up, even though that's of utmost significance for us, but additionally it means that <u>we will see God in others and in their situations.</u> <u>We will</u> <u>have discernment and see how He sees them and we will see His love for them and how He is working in their lives. It also</u> <u>means we will see their shortcomings, but without any personal judgement against them. We will have His heart.</u>

When our hearts are n<u>ot pure, we will be in idolatry, affected by</u> <u>our biases, our emotions, our judgments and think we are seeing the truth because God will allow this error in us because we have</u> <u>not chosen the way of love.</u> When we don't love others, we will be blind, which means we can't see what's wrong and we will<u> be left in</u> <u>our deception.</u> He expects us to examine our own lives and see how it lines up with His Word, with the fruit of the Spirit and with His love and to be Doers of the Word.

I now can see that all His commandments are but a part of love. After we have practiced obeying His Word and have overcome our flesh, we don't have to think of the commandments anymore, because they all come together in LOVE and LOVE fulfills all of His requirements - all of the law. AND, now as I read 1 Cor 14, I realize that the power of His perfect love needs to be the motivating force for all the other gifts in our lives also, because <u>all wisdom and power is included in His love in us</u> and through us.

Faith works by love.

When His love dwells in us, we have <u>no more doubts about our Father's intention or ability</u> to lead us in His perfect ways. We learn to <u>trust Him fully because we know who He</u> is. We can <u>enter into His rest because we do not have anything to fear</u>. We've come to <u>know how perfectly He does all things, how</u> <u>wise He is in all His ways, how pure His love is, how faithful He is</u> <u>and how He cannot lie.</u> As for God, <u>His way is perfect and it leads us perfectly to Him and to the perfect fulfillment of His purpose in</u> <u>our lives</u>. His ways, as we obey, do perfect those things that concern us. In the end, we will be amazed at how <u>our lives are so fully</u> <u>aligned with His Word and with His heart and will.</u>

As we become doers of every commandment of the Lord, <u>each commandment has a part in helping prepare us to be His</u> habitation, <u>His overcomers, His manifested sons, His Bride, because obeying His commandments has killed our flesh</u>.

Because of our intimacy with the Lord, <u>our obedience is in Spirit and Truth</u> - not the letter of the law that brings self righteousness and puts us back under the curse and death. The Word tells us not to lean to our own understanding, but in all our ways we are to acknowledge Him. (see Proverbs 3) However, this is not possible for us unless we become doers of the Word because we only know how to live by our own understanding, but being Doers of the Word renews our minds and develops in us the Mind of Christ.

Our natural man only knows how to eat from the Tree of Knowledge until we are saved by faith in Jesus who is the Tree of Life, but it's only as we obey Him continually in all things that we will be eating of that Tree. And it's only then that the River of Life will freely flow out of us to others that they might live. (Ezek 47:9)

Abraham obeyed God to leave his country and family Hebrews 11-8 NLT By faith Abraham, when called to go to a place he would later receive as his inheritance, obeyed and went,<u> even</u> though he did not know where he was going.- We also as Abraham's seed and heirs according to the promise are often called to obey God's voice not knowing where it will take us or where we are going. <u>When</u>

<u>God was teaching me how to hear His voice and walk in obedience to trust Him that His ways for me were Perfect,</u>

<u>I had no idea of where it would take me.</u> I had no idea <u>He was</u> <u>forming His Kingdom in me of righteousness, peace and (eventually) joy</u>. I just obeyed. It is so beautiful the way God does things because it has nothing to do with our efforts so no wild beast (pride) can overtake us.

Men's ways of loving and living are a complete opposite to God's kind of loving and living. There is no similarity at all to His kind of love. But in the keeping of His commandments, we discover the secret of our transformation, that is, <u>He is the Word made flesh, so when we submit to His Word, we are submitting to</u> <u>Him, and He is going to live His life through us.</u> It will no longer be us, but Him living in us.

To begin with, who would imagine that God would say that the love of God is to keep His commandments. To the natural man, these two entities do not seem to be related at all. <u>Until we actually</u> <u>start keeping His commandments, we can't have the revelation of this truth.</u>

<u>**The prophets have told me that I would be imparting Love**</u> <u>**and Life to the Body**</u> so I have been <u>learning what God's definition</u> <u>of love is and practicing it </u>in every situation in my life. I always KNEW that the gifts of Love and Life which the Lord said I would bring, had to be very significant but I am continually learning to this day just what

love and life really are, and the all encompassing role they must play in our spiritual walk. These gifts must be developed but can only be produced by God. There is no other source. They cannot come from our own efforts, and most certainly not through religious practices.

Love brings us a lot of pain because no greater love can we have than to lay down our lives for others. Love always costs us something. Love always comes from the heart. Through trials, troubles and pain is the gateway to greater revelation of Him to reveal Himself to you.

As we continue to love through it all, His love in us will be refined, purified, and empowered to break through peoples' defenses. Love is indeed as strong as death - it is the greatest gift and it never fails.Whereas man's kind of love is always Selfish. - Even when it appears unselfish like sacrificing for someone, the word says if it's without love it profits us nothing. How can our "unselfish" giving be selfish? Sometimes we do it out of guilt, or to make ourselves look good or feel good or to take pride in what we've done.

One prophet shared: -"A witness is arising on this earth and they are my full grown sons and daughters. They have my fire in their eyes, the <u>fire of my pure holy love in their hearts, and they</u> <u>have my pure holy love pouring from their lips.</u>

<u>"Soon, the whole world will understand, LOVE</u> <u>NEVER</u> <u>FAILS!</u> Do you hear my words oh heavens, do you hear my words oh earth, LOVE NEVER

FAILS AND PERFECT LOVE CASTS OUT ALL FEAR."

There's a time when all your trials are meant to kill your flesh and humble you, but then <u>there comes a time when Love is matured in you and trials don't kill your flesh anymore because you have become love and filled with compassion for the accuser. You have a continual feast of good things because you see everyone through God's eyes. You see how all things you've been through have been for good. Your heart and mind are at rest in His faithfulness and wisdom.</u>

The pure in heart shall see God! I have learned that it's only after we have obeyed God's Word that we will get the true and fuller revelation of God. He hides the revelation and it doesn't get released until the required obedience is fulfilled. So that's why at the end, there are so many Suddenlies! The last click of the combination on the lock springs it open or the last drop of rain causes an overflow.

The Harvest in my life is now pouring in so quickly it's hard to fathom. And I know it has nothing to do with my efforts or abilities - He has shown me through the years that it's ALL HIM! All I had to do was BELIEVE HIM and OBEY HIM and He made my way perfect for me to accomplish His Will.

Prophet Russ Walden wrote: "The Father says today, <u>be rooted and grounded in My love. Let My love be the open expanse above you and the foundation under your feet. My love is loving you and prospering you.</u> My love is making all things

48

work together for your good. <u>My love is ruling and reigning over every circumstance in your life. My love is rearranging ands reconstituting the fullness of My promise</u>, even in areas where you have despaired of ever having anything different than what you were experiencing. Step out into that love this day, says the Father. Launch out into the hope that love sustains and maintains. I am marking your life with My love and it is a good life and an abundant life even beyond your expectations.

"Are you prepared to be radically loved, says the Father?

"I have shown My loving kindness so often that at times it went unnoticed. <u>My love is so full that at times it seems monolithic and featureless because I refused to allow My love to be interrupted or marred by anything else but love.</u> Stop for a moment and breathe in. That is Me loving you. Breathe out and you are experiencing Me loving you. Look out of your eyes and take in your surroundings and in so doing you are experiencing My unconditional love. "Make up your mind that you will not see yourself as anything other than a child that is loved and accepted. You are clamoring for approval and you haven't figured out just how much I accept you already.

"<u>If all the people of the world were dead to self and serving each other through the power of God's love then there would not be a needy person in this world</u>", says the Spirit of God.

"My Son came to set the perfect example but most are appalled and offended at that example. <u>Love is not just spoken, IT IS LOVE DEMONSTRATED.</u>

"This is My heart for people and this is what I am calling you to. I have been <u>looking for a people of love</u>—those who will love the unlovely and the outcasts just as I did.

"Loose the Power of Love - First within your own lives - Begin in your language ... For out of the heart the mouth speaks, then let it permeate your entire being ... Your motivations ... Your actions ... Your intentions. Then the Power of Love will flow from you as you pour it out towards others The **Power of Love is what the world** <u>seeks but cannot find</u>." **//** End

The Word says that there is <u>no law against love</u> - I am learning just what that means and it is so liberating! When we love the Lord and all others across our path, we do not have to wonder if we have done the right thing. Love is the final thing. When we show God's love (by the Spirit) we've done all that is right. The beginning of wisdom is the fear of the Lord which causes us to fully obey God's commandments by His grace, however, the end of wisdom is love, because to love is so wise, so powerful, - as strong as death.

<u>Prophetic Words re LOVE (authors unknown):</u>

"<u>Love is the wisdom for those that reject the Lord</u>. -<u>Love will</u> <u>break the strongholds, break through the lies, and bestow blessings</u> <u>on entire nations where religion has constantly failed them.</u> Love will be the answer as it's always been and see us through to the end, but it has to be God's love and not our own sentiments of what we think love is.

"Both a <u>season of great blessing and intense difficulty</u> are being used by God to prepare a people to take a forever step into the deep Spirit mist of <u>God's glorious mystery life of **TOTAL LOVE.**</u>

"Pure holy love is the core ingredient of abundant quality life in this world. **Health, well-being, prosperity, righteous-ness, peace, joy, and every good quality of life - comes by LOVE.**

"ALL THINGS IN GOD'S KINGDOM ARE ORDERED BY LOVE! ALL OF THE LAW IS FULFILLED BY PURE HOLY LOVE.

"<u>Power and wisdom come through love.</u> <u>Wisdom comes from</u> <u>heaven through the love</u> <u>connection with God</u> as the <u>light of God</u> <u>flows to our hearts</u> on earth. <u>The greatest motivational force on earth is love</u>. Only for love will one lay down his life for another. Only for the love of God will we willingly lay down our life as crucified with Christ. It is by love that we are drawn to lose our self-life and enter into the far greater life in God and Him in us in Christ Jesus by the Holy Spirit."

Susan Vercelli: "This is what the Lord said. As you have endured rejection with extreme prejudice, so you shall <u>rejoice in extreme acceptance without prejudice!</u> You will<u> enjoy abundance in</u> <u>every aspect of your life</u> as you are blessed by My Spirit, and everyone will see it!"

Wanda Algers "The **<u>day of perfect pure holy love is here and</u> <u>my full grown sons and daughters will walk in the fullness of</u> <u>that love</u>** and they will demonstrate my love words, my love's actions and my love's judgments on the earth and in my house. Judgment begins in the house of the Lord.

"**<u>I am judging everything by the standard of my pure holy</u> <u>love</u>**. That which is not pure holy love will be burned up and removed so only that which is birthed in and from my pure holy love can remain. There is no fear in love.

"So rejoice my sons and daughters, **<u>I am releasing my "firebrands"</u>** to go forth to reclaim what is mine and to go in and possess the land that I have given them. No one shall withstand them for as I was with Moses so am I with them.

"Their going forth is **like the dawning of the new day.** Today I declare that this word is now fulfilled in your ears. The rising of my firebrands is now here and the nations are going to tremble at my appearance within them.

"The earth has never seen such a people and they will never see such a people like my <u>full grown sons and daughters who will</u> <u>now inherit the earth.</u>

"So hear my words oh heavens, hear my words oh earth. Arise my sons and daughters, arise my fire brands **you will now come into your divine assignments and you will go forth to every tribe and every nation and you will bring forth my end time sons and daughters** into my Kingdom.

"<u>You will bring forth my will on Earth as it is heaven. So hear the word of the Lord. Fire brands I call you forth today.</u> You will come together, the dry bones shall now live and be seen upon the earth. Blessed are the people whose God is the Lord." end

<u>Love enables us to</u> <u>Speak the Truth -</u> It means all of the nature and character of Christ is resident in us and fully compliant with the Word and it is He who is speaking through us with His love.

To worship in spirit and truth means the same - that we worship Him in a full and accurate revelation of who he is - and everything in us has been brought to agreement with His Word so that our worship is given **with a pure, sincere heart of love.**

One could say we have become naturally spiritual - having the character and love of Christ ruling from within. Gone are the days of *"trying"*, *"practicing"*, *"contending"* - at last we partake of the Harvest and get to experience the life of Christ becoming a reality within our own lives. <u>I am experiencing the love, joy and peace of His life continually now.</u> **He has become my life,** my nature, and it is not an effort to manifest Him. The "expected end" we've been told about finally is manifested. There is a beginning and an end. His promises and words are completely true and we have only to believe and obey.

Love produces MATURE FRUIT

But the fruit of the Spirit

[the result of His presence within us] is love [unselfish concern for others], joy, [inner] peace, patience [not the ability to wait, but how we act while waiting], kindness, goodness, faithfulness, gentleness, self-control. Against such things there is no law. (Galatians 5: 22-23, AMP)

There is only one place in all the kingdoms where equality of races, equality of haves and have nots and equality of men and women exists; and that place is "in Christ". (read Galatians 3:28) And being "in Christ" is not a religion, it is not a doctrine, it is not just a promise, but it's the reality and destination for all those who are willing to die to themselves as they walk and live in God's commandments (which are the seeds of life) and those seeds mature and produce after their own kind; which, in this case, produces "Christ" in us.

When a person submits to God and obeys His commands and ways, it will always bring them to the death of themselves so that they can declare in reality, "It is no longer I that liveth but Christ dwells in me". It is only after that point in a Christian's life that he/she can walk in the true liberty of the equality and freedom provided for us. Prior to that death, the reality of equality and freedom are only things we believe and can press towards but we cannot claim them to be our present reality.

By faith we can call our "seeds" by their fruit's name, but we can't eat the fruit itself or share it with others yet until the fruit actually matures and ripens. (One summer all of my loquats on my trees were nice and orange and large but when I asked the Lord how I could tell when they were ripe, He said I could press them and the ripe ones would be tender. What a difference it made when I picked the tender ones. They tasted so good and juicy and the texture was excellent. All the loquats were real loquats, but I got to eat ones that were fully ripe and that contained the fullness of the qualities a loquat is intended to have.)

And so it is that when others can taste Christ in us it is because we can walk in the freedom and equality provided for us. The Word tells us that the day will come when God would seek those who worship Him in spirit and truth. Jesus is the truth, the Word is the truth, but **we are not of that truth until we die to ourselves** and we are totally transformed to be like Him, having His same Spirit. We can only have faith that it will happen until it does.

Chapter 4

Naturally Spiritual

In the flesh area of our lives, we are told to take up our cross daily, but in those areas where the work of the cross has produced peace and overcoming, it is time to walk in resurrection life - because now Christ lives in us. This is the point when the righteous are bold as a lion. This is the time when our "resting" in Him is being seated with Him on a throne of authority. In Christ we see that we are neither male nor female but a new creature. It's a time of discovery and reality.

We are told that our faith in the Lord is counted as Righteousness, and this is essential to practice that faith. But there comes a time that the faith produces righteous character and righteous works that are seen.

How awesome it is to become **"naturally" spiritual** - having the character and love of Christ ruling and flowing from within as your new nature - as your new default. Gone are the days of only "trying", "practicing", "contending" (all of which are necesary) - at last we partake of the Harvest and get to experience the life of Christ becoming a reality within our own lives. Others may not believe that I am living this new life of Christ in me, but I am experiencing the love, joy and peace of His life continually now. He has become my life, my nature and it is not an effort to manifest Him; He manifests Himself. The "expected end" we've been told about finally is manifesting. There is a beginning and an end. His promises and His Word are completely true and we have only to believe and obey to experience the ultimate manifestation.

It's fine when a Christian talks about the promises in the Bible, or recounts the testimonies of others, but it's often very offensive to people when that Christian says that the promises have been made manifest in their own life - today, saying "This is what God has done for me."

But there is no other result we can have when we are Doers of the Word because every word is a Seed, and when we plant that seed into the good soil of our lives through faith and obedience, practicing living the Word, it produces the fruit that was intended - fruit after its own kind. To the one who has not been a Doer of the Word but a Hearer only, this sounds almost heretical, outrageous or worse because they've never experienced this manifestation and interpret it as being "pride" on the part of the one testifying of the faithfulness of God.

But if we're willing to let the seed of our life die and fall into the ground, there comes a time when that seed produces a new life and It's no longer a behavior we put on according to tradition and religion, even the law. As we learn to walk in His Ways, He takes up residence in us, He takes over, our life becomes His, and He manifests Himself through us - especially speaking with His voice through us - His love and life flowing through us. It's no longer the "I" in us that lives, but it is Christ living in and through us, because we've died to our own will and ego. Now we love others through His love and we're not just trying to love them. We give out of the overflow of His heart in us and not just dutifully or out of sympathy. Because we've become love, it means we automatically fulfill His commandments.

Like Adam and Eve, we have learned to become naked and not ashamed. No more hiding from God but we've learned to speak the truth in love to Him, to others and to ourselves.

He will now have freedom to speak and express Himself through us, even though people will ask "Who do you think you are?"

> *Wherefore I take pleasure in weaknesses, in injuries, in necessities, in persecutions, in distresses, for Christ's sake: for when I am weak, then am I strong.* (2 Corinthians 12:10, American Standard Version ASV)

There are times the Lord protects us from a storm, and there are times He requires us to speak to the storm…and then there are times that He simply gives us the strength to ride out the storm as we stand on the Word.

> *a land which Jehovah thy God careth for: the eyes of Jehovah thy God are always upon it, from the beginning of the year even unto the end of the year. And it shall come to pass, if ye shall hearken diligently unto my commandments which I command you this day, to love Jehovah your God, and to serve him with all your heart and with all your soul,* (Deuteronomy 11:12-13, American Standard Version ASV)

Many Christians do not believe the Old Testament is relevant to our day, but Jesus said He didn't come to destroy the law but to fulfill it. Again we have to go and learn what that means, which I did. - I've learned that we can never earn the blessings of God through any righteousness or effort of our own, but as we obey Him to believe, He gives us a brand new heart and He writes His laws on it and takes us on a path where He is able to keep working in us to Will and Do of His good pleasure - which positions us for all blessings and increase and fulfillment of His promises.

Chapter 5

New Beginning - Enlarging My Territory:

New Home:

A year after my husband's death in 2013, the Lord had me purchase a lavish, retreat-style home in the Sierra Foothills (now called "Eagles Retreat".) It is beyond anything I could ever imagine that I would live in, so I waited for the confirmation of a few prophets to convince me that this really was for me. One prophet even told me this house was built for me, and I have to admit that I love living here and it blesses me totally.

The Lord said that we must believe that He is, and that He is a Rewarder of those who diligently seek Him, so I had been practicing believing that for decades, in the midst of laying down my life, but still this was overwhelming. (see Hebrews 11)

Knowing my Father, however, I knew there was more to this than just being a reward and blessing for me...And prophets began to confirm that to me, saying that this would be a place of His Glory where eagles would gather and that would touch people's lives with peace, healing, restoration, love and joy. He has especially let me know that He will be bringing many leaders here to be ministered to. - He said some would be on the level of Billy Graham and Oral Roberts. He said I was an apostle to apostles, a general to generals, a leader to leaders, a mother to the mothers and fathers.

When the Lord told me to buy this 5000 sq ft lavish home I'm living in, I was shocked and wondered why He would have me do this. Religion would tell us that there are so many poor people and that we shouldn't have lavish homes so that we would have more to give. But I've learned that Yes, we should have the heart to give and not to indulge ourselves, but also that God has higher Kingdom purposes that He is establishing and we have to remember not to lean to our own understanding if we are going to allow Him to do His will in our lives. Jesus said that <u>the poor you will always have with you, but I believe He was saying that - "right now the Father is doing something else"</u>.

In my early years the Lord told me to always remember that He loved me as much as He loved anyone He would send me to. If He wants me to live in Paradise on earth as it is in heaven - now in this season, (so that He can show the world

His Kingdom and how faithful He is, and that His Word is true), what is that to me? I have given myself fully to Him and gone through the decades of fiery trials, so at this time in my walk, He has prepared me to be able to enjoy His rich blessings in glory without taking it to myself, and He wants me to enable others to experience the riches He has for them. I do not know what lies ahead and I am not promoting an idol of everyone being wealthy, but the Lord wants us to know there's a time and place for wealth in our lives when we walk uprightly. It is part of His covenant promises.

If we live by the letter of the law and decline God's blessings, it can make us very religious. For example, I met a missionary who had been ministering and sacrificing his life for 20 years in the Orient. When I met him I really wanted to bless him for all he had sacrificed, and I did. However, one day when he came to visit me, he saw a nice watch that my son had bought me and he tapped his finger on it as if to say "Why do you have an expensive watch? - Don't you know you should have sold it and given the money to the poor?"

Yes, I know one of God's commandments is to give to the poor, but He also says He wants to bless us, and I felt a grieving of my spirit because His religious spirit was what was grieving God at that moment. When we live in intimacy and obedience to the Lord, we will have the discernment we need.

After 3 years of living up here in the Sierra Foothills, I have come to realize several things.

1. God wanted to **enlarge my thinking.** I was told years ago that I had a "littleness of mind". Now I can understand what He meant and now I am seeing it enlarged and know that word was true. The Lord wants us to fully appreciate who He is, and what we are created to be, but first He has to reduce us to ground O in our natural self and that takes a lot of work on God's part, and trust on ours. If He doesn't kill our flesh, then He could not do this enlarging for us because we would take pride in ourselves and it would ruin everything. God wants to give us our full reward and blessing, but He has to wait for our cooperation so He can build a right foundation that will stand in the face of temptation and trials so that His blessings won't destroy us. He wants us to experience all of the love He has for us so we can have a revelation of our value to Him and of who we really are. We have to know the love of God in order to love ourselves and in order to love others as we ought.

2. When we cooperate fully with God's processes and keep praising Him through sufferings, thanking Him for the perfect work He's doing in us, He will build something **beautiful** in our lives beyond our comprehension. And what I love is that there is no need to "try" to stay humble, because the process strips you of pride and you

KNOW that it was all God and not you. Stripping and crushing are totally necessary because what He is building in us is so huge that we could not withstand the weight and pressure of it if we were not prepared by His delivering us from living by our own strength.

This home is an earthly example of the beauty of heaven to me. It is so far beyond anything I imagined to live in and it has such beauty in the architecture and landscaping - in the trees, flowers, pond, waterfall, etc., such quality of materials and construction. Every morning I awaken to all this surrounding beauty and it overwhelms me every day.

3. The Lord said He will be sending me leaders of the highest rank in His kingdom, of commerce and government. Although He deposits His life in all believers, we all have a different part and somehow the Lord has deposited a fullness of His life uniquely in me so that I can impart it to others. This home is a haven of rest and peace and many will receive healing and restoration and it is already happening, so this is another purpose God had in placing me here in this Eagles Retreat).

New Life

Our New Life positions us differently from the old. In the old life, we had to fight the enemy, but now we have authority over him because we are seated above him, putting him under our feet and treading him under and taking back all he stole from us - and more.

We are not just claiming something we believe or that is written, but we speak from a real experience and personal knowledge. We have been delivered to become deliverers of others; saved, to be saviors on Mt. Zion. The curse causeless cannot alight on us.

We are no longer contending for God's blessings and provision, but we are confident in His promises and calling them forth. We have an expected end. We KNOW that because our God is faithful and good, that we will never fail to receive His promises,

He rewards, and He even tells us that we MUST BELIEVE that He is and that He is a rewarder of those who seek Him. Everything will indeed work together for our Good and we will never be ashamed or disappointed. We have been circumcised and now we have no more confidence in ourselves but all our confidence is in Him.

We are the Bride coming out of the wilderness, leaning on her Beloved. He is now being made perfect in our weakness so we go from strength to strength and glory to glory, daily experiencing more and more of His Promises.

Our eyes are single so our bodies are becoming full of light. This light not only illumines us but it empowers us and positions us. Others see this light in us shining forth and we are growing in favor with God and man; His presence in us causes His voice to be heard and to be released through us. The righteous are indeed becoming bold as a lion - tearing down strongholds, opening prison doors and setting captives free; opening blinded eyes and causing them to see.

We are tasting and seeing how good God is. We are satisfied as we see how He has caused us to be conformed to His image, to be in His likeness. The fruit of our lives looks like the kind of seed that was planted - it has produced after its kind.

It's no longer the I that lives, but it's now Christ living in us who causes us to be able to do all things through His strength. Now that we're in Christ, we experience what it is to no longer just be male and female, but a new creature. We also experience the freedom from cultural confinement, prejudices, limitations and curses.

We are NEW creatures in every way. Our outward circumstances do not affect who we are. Whether we are a business owner or the janitor at the business, we are still reigning, we are still victorious, full of His love, peace and joy.

No weapon formed against us can prosper. The fiery darts hurled against us, fall to the ground and are consumed. There is no more condemnation or guilt - we are washed in the blood of the Lamb and our sins that were scarlet are now white as snow. Love has been made perfect and has cast out all fear. His love in and through us causes us to fulfill all of the law, so that no curse will alight upon us, because Jesus became that curse for us.

We know that we will finish the race because we can do it through Christ; we know we won't be ashamed or disappointed because it is finished. Christ not only paid the price for us to be saved, but we are now saved by His life in us. He is our all in all and we are bone of His bone and flesh of His flesh, and He who began a good work in us will surely complete it; He will perfect that which concerns us. He will continue to work in us to will and do His good pleasure.

We have come to believe that He is a rewarder of those that diligently seek Him. He is the God who works all things together for our GOOD and He even gives us the desires of our heart because we have become one with His heart and His desires, His will. We have come to see that <u>everything He allows in our lives is out of His</u> <u>love for us and to bring us to the fullness of our destiny in Him.</u> He has called us with purpose, and He also prepares and equips us to fulfill it and to bring Him glory. We are not a people who will take the glory to ourselves, nor do we have any desire to do so.

Our cup runs over with joy as we realize He will bring us over the Finish Line and that <u>nothing can deter us or stop us. It is no</u> <u>longer possible for us to be deceived because as we have obeyed</u> <u>His Word, He has come to run the race in us.</u> He has given His angels charge over us and His precious Holy Spirit empowers us, teaches us, quickens us and leads us.

When we are weak we are strong for His strength is made perfect in our weakness. He has painstakingly <u>brought us to the place of a broken and contrite heart</u> so that we could take His yoke upon us and be meek and lowly as He is - so that His strength and His authority are ours and made perfect in our weakness. He gives His grace to the humble so as He has humbled us, His grace is sufficient for us and enables us to do all things according to the Father's will. His grace is our enablement because it's not by might nor by power, but by His Spirit.

We didn't know that every commandment that we obeyed instead of doing our own will was <u>allowing Him to become our all in all </u>because He is the Word and we are surrendering our will to Him. His throne is being established in our lives every time we submit to His will, and because He sits on His throne and reigns over all, we are delivered from all evil and His fiery sword is now in our mouths because we have come to rule and reign with Him.

We have come to be **partakers of His life, and** we are gladly <u>willing to **partake of His sufferings that we might have His glory** resting on us </u>and filling us. We are a <u>people who love not our own lives unto death</u>, because we have practiced rejoicing in all trials and tribulations through which we have entered His Kingdom and have become those violent ones who have taken it by force. We continually decree, "Come Thy Kingdom and be done Thy Will - on earth (and in me) as it is in heaven." Because we truly love the Father, we do not love the world or any of its lusts or affections. We have died to the world and the world to us. We live for Him alone - our eye has become singled to Him - we have no other lovers. He is our sole satisfaction.

We have died and no longer live, so now He lives through us. He is made wisdom and revelation to us and He is our righteousness, our redeemer, the author and finisher of our faith, the alpha and omega, the beginning and the end and He is perfecting that which concerns us so that we will be part of the Bride who has prepared herself and made herself ready.

There is no good thing our God withholds from us. He IS, and He is a rewarder of those who seek Him. He gives us a harvest of all we have sown and restores all the enemy has stolen from us over the years, even seven-fold. Because we love Him, He gives us the desires of our heart so that we are fully satisfied in our lives. He shares His heart and His mind with us, even giving us **His Spirit without measure** as we have given our lives to Him without limit. He gives us every good and perfect gift so that we can accomplish His will. He is with us always so we are never lonely, but also He sets us in families that we might bless and support one another in the Body, and He gives us **prepared leaders (mothers and fathers**) who train us, strengthen us and help provide for us.

As Jesus <u>endured the cross for the joy </u>set before Him, <u>we</u> <u>have learned also to endure our trials for the exceeding joy that is </u><u>ours. His joy has become our strength. We have learned to rejoice</u> <u>always</u> and to give thanks in all things. We have learned that though the tears endured for the night that joy did indeed come in the morning. <u>We are blessed with beauty for our ashes, with faith</u> <u>that is more precious than fine gold.</u>

The same Spirit that raised Christ from the dead dwells in us, and AS HE RAISED Christ from the dead, so **He is also raising us up and quickening our mortal bodies.** He is our resurrection life and power and we are walking in the newness of life. We are experiencing the restoration of our lives and learning to overcome all death, so that we are victorious and putting all our enemies under our feet. And because we are those who have overcome we are being given the right to be seated with Christ on His throne at the right hand of God and reigning with Him as His people who are called, chosen and faithful. We know that we shall inherit ALL things! even if we don't yet know what all those things are because the Word says our eyes haven't seen, nor have our ears heard, nor have they entered our heart - the things God has prepared for us who love Him - which means those who keep His commandments.

Keeping His commandments is a matter of our love for the Lord and wanting Him to have His way in us, which means we will be more and more in the likeness of His Son.

We are not keeping His commandments to earn righteousness - that would only <u>end up with our being Self Righteous and put us under the law of sin and death and under the curse</u> again. <u>Yes it actually can bring a curse upon us</u> if we depend on our own performance of obeying the law to be saved because the Word says "Gal 3:10, that all who rely on the works of the law are under a curse,"

This speaks of keeping the letter of the law to gain righteousness as opposed to obeying the Word because we are yielded and obedient to the Lord in intimacy.

> *I have been crucified with Christ; and it is no longer I that live, but Christ liveth in me: and that life which I now live in the flesh I live in faith, the faith which is in the Son of God, who loved me, and gave himself up for me.* (Galatians 2:20, American Standard Version ASV)

When we first get saved, as we read the Word, it is a wonder and a discovery of truth, then as we start growing, we apply the appropriate Word when it is needed and practice believing it, bu**t there comes a time, when we believe with our whole hearts and begin to proclaim it because it has become a reality** in our lives. <u>We become that</u>

<u>Word and the Word is made flesh in us</u> and the Word is Christ. At some point there is <u>no more "trying" or "practicing" to do or become, but it is!</u> It is impossible for us to grow fruits of the Spirit in our lives, but as <u>we plant the seed of God's Word in our lives, that seed produces fruit after its kind</u>; we become one of the many <u>b</u><u>rethren of whom Christ was the firstfruits. </u>Through our faith and obedience, God produces the fruit and gives us the increase. It is <u>not by any of our own efforts</u>.

I started my walk with God, believing it was impossible for me to be like Him, having the fruit of the Spirit. But through the years, I could see He was changing me, and now I can say<u> His fruits have become manifest in my life. They are who I am now. </u>and He continues to perfect His fruit in me. It is such a pleasure and blessing to become more and more like Him. It tastes so good! and it's a sweet smelling aroma to the Lord, and it's all Him.

> *[a]Owe nothing to anyone except to [b]love and seek the best for one another; for he who [unselfishly] loves his neighbor has fulfilled the [essence of the] law [relating to one's fellowman].* (Romans 13:8, Amplified Bible AMP)

What I love about God's Ways in particular is that they are <u>all</u> <u>about His wisdom, His power and His faithfulness in our lives. It's</u> <u>not up to us to</u>

produce the fruit of the Spirit, we can't. We have only to do one thing - that is to obey Him, and He does the rest.

He takes us in a path uniquely designed for each of us - we will encounter the right people, the right circumstances, the right timing that God will use together for our good, to this end.

Chapter 6

New Creativity

I have experienced more new things in my life now that I am in my 80's than ALL my previous years put together. When I was in my mid 70's I thought I shouldn't dance before the Lord anymore, but a prophet had a vision of me dancing so I kept going, and I think that permission to not stop dancing at that age, gave me an impetus to push on.

I have practiced obeying God and His word for almost 50 years, but I **also was believing His promises** that He is the same yesterday, today and always. I saw all the amazing things He has done for His people who obeyed Him and I've been expecting to experience those types of things too. So in my mind, I'm not totally surprised at all that it's happening, but at the same time, it's still so amazing because it's so much and so far beyond me. And I know I've only begun - there's so much more.

Decorating Home:

When I moved into my new paradise, I looked at all the assorted pieces of furniture I owned and had no idea of where to put anything. My husband had never been open to the idea of my developing a style of decorating, so I never had the opportunity to make decorating decisions before and this was a real challenge. As with everything else though, I began to pray about it and it was so wonderful how things began to fall into place and how many times He actually showed me what to do - in addition to sending me help from others of course - especially my youngest son.

A couple of times He even woke me up in the middle of the night and told me where to put things. And those choices were so perfect. There were also times I made mistakes and had to learn a lesson from it, but recently I have become more creative and sometimes even bold to attempt new things, or correct mistakes.

I am still growing in this area but I don't feel defeated anymore when I try new things. Instead I have grace to continually grow.

Creating Mini Landscapes

I am finding that the Lord can make us creative. My disciple Todd had been a macho man who had never dabbled in the arts. But when someone gave him some art supplies he began creating wooden art pieces and he enjoyed making these so much that in his great generous heart, he wanted to include me. He brought over a couple of his driftwood flower containers he had sculpted and I had the experience and great joy of filling them with nature's dried flowers and rocks. It was so rewarding and it looks so beautiful on my dining table. Someone already told me that if someone saw this like on a table in a restaurant, he could see them wanting to buy it. Of course it was not mainly about the monetary value, but hearing the aesthetic value it had to him, that he thought it was beautiful, really blessed me. God is restoring my soul and enlarging me.

Recording CD

Who would have ever thought that I would be making a professionally recorded CD? The Lord showed Jacques Cook that He wanted him to make a CD with me, even though I am not a professional musician in any way, but he is. The Lord told him that he and I had the same frequency in worship - the same weight. Also the recording was made in one session even, which I was told was not common for a novice, which was definitely by God's grace and favor! The owner of the studio is not a Christian but he said he was inspired by it and that he got goosebumps which he said rarely happens to him.

Even so, it was hard for me to understand why the Lord wanted this recording. What was its value to people? I didn't know how to describe the CD to anyone when they asked, and at first I was even afraid to listen to it myself. But finally when I listened, I was surprisingly blessed and relieved at what I heard. I appreciate this one woman's comment, "I was not just listening to a CD — it was a beautiful experience." And when Jacques told me that God had Anointed my voice, I began to understand more. All the prophetic words to me were beginning to come together.

The Lord has said "I'm giving My people a 'million-dollar' voice this year. It won't be just saying the right words but how they say it. Speaking from a right spirit will produce million-dollar results."

Finances/Properties

My oldest sons said he thought I had some unhealthy fears that negatively influenced my financial decisions, and I agreed with him and knew it was true. I have made many mistakes (as far as man's understanding is concerned) but praise the Lord, He knows our shortcomings and He uses them for good as He heals us, teaches us and delivers us from them. I now have so much more peace and freedom in my finances and this new confidence is helping me to hear and see more

<u>clearly so that I can take necessary steps to set things in order</u>.

I have found it <u>a joy to give now but I also have expectation that what I've sown I will</u> <u>also reap</u>. I have expectation that all the promises the Lord has given me about my having great wealth will be fulfilled because He's given me a heart to want to help others and that takes money!

I thank the Lord that it is He who is leading me and that He is covenanted with me to teach me, restore me, and to supply my needs, whether through people, investments or supernaturally.

I have mostly chosen to invest in God's sons and daughters who are giving their all for the Lord - those who are obedient and who learn to love. but the Lord told me that they would in turn one day look after me. That is very comforting.

When I look back over the years I realize that many times I had desired to buy certain properties but was not given the opportunity to do it. But now, at the Lord's leading, I own not only a beautiful home, but He has allowed me to buy a prayer house nearby with a creek and a large wooded lot that needs a lot of work to prepare for those disciples He has promised to send me. It has great potential and I'm excited about it, because it is particularly significant that he sent just the RIGHT, UNIQUE SON to help me develop the property. Our Father has built a real mother/son relationship between us and His House is being built with wisdom and love.

Chapter 7

Ministry

Mother in Zion

As I have shared the testimonies of many disciples, you can see that the Lord has blessed me to be a Mother in Zion to true Sons and Daughters and as I have been called to be a part of helping prepare them for their powerful destinies in God, we have truly become a Family, because they are being trained with "the Truth in Love" that God has formed in me and wants for every one of us.

Being a Mother or Father in the Lord is not about a "position" over others, just expecting to be honored by them, nor is it about just coddling them, but it's about being an example of walking in humility and obedience and faithfulness to God, demonstrating maturity and the wisdom of God and showing His love and truth and discipline to each son and daughter He gives me; so that they in turn learn to express honor and respect to others. I've learned to be patient, but firm and yet flexible.

This is a word I received in 2011: "I've <u>called you to **mother** young men</u> <u>and bring them into the fold,</u> those who have a heart for ministry, those that I've called, but they **need that mothering, they need that sternness and discipline you can give them.**

<u>Some will have to be housed</u> because they have no place to go, but He says "I'm working that out" and<u> **you'll have a facility where** **they can grow -**</u> where yo<u>u can house</u> the young men; I'm not saying there won't be women, but I'm hearing that **God has called you to raise up the men, and t**hey will call you Mother now. Some of <u>My sons have never had a mother's love and have never been close</u> or had understanding, because all their lives they had to fight. But<u> He'll show them the love of God - the **mother love of God in** you - and you will **balance them.**</u> Don't change what you're doing because it's been Me; You pray and cry and fast for the people God sends to you, I see people just showing up on your doorstep. You ask, "Where did you come from?"<u> and **I see these people coming because you have the heart,** and God says 'The enemy will also send some but **you'll discern who to bring in and who cannot** come in;</u> He's got that covering over you, and He says Continue to mother, because you are a seer; and you have a prophetic voice, but you also have an **apostolic mantle to build up and send**

out; it has nothing to do with age because I give you long life.

"You will begin to teach and raise up entrepreneurs; Wealth and **riches are your portion.** You know how to handle wealth because you have wealth already and I can trust you. You'll have such an anointing on your life that I've already placed in you and it'll begin to stir. You'll have such a vision, creative ideas, that you're going to release and impart it unto them. They'll implement the vision and begin to run with it, but they will always remember where they got it from, and they'll always come back and pour back into your life."

The dream that Krista Shirley had is a great description of what God is doing: "A Birthing of Greatness/A Purging of Toxicity -excerpts (you can see full Blog)

"I live my life with so many unique and interesting supernatural happenings and this just adds to the collection. Papa showed me that I and many others have <u>birthed a big baby</u>. This baby will <u>produce generations of strong, mighty and **powerful supergiants** </u> all over the earth. These giants will not just be individual warriors but <u>will be **united together to form one alliance of peace and power.**</u> As I was meditating on this wondrous happening, Papa reminded me of my ancestry. I'm from a tribe of the Iroquois Indians and while they were reigning, they were known as a tribe of "Power & Peace"!

I strongly feel that these supergiants **will be full of power and** peace to help restore the earth and bring it back into order.

"They will also show the **greatest level of love** that has been shown to the world to prove Papa's heart for this world. Another amazing description of these supergiants would be, "Love warriors teaching **peace and justice** throughout the world." I see these warriors **bringing unity** where no one thought it was possible and this will cause the greatest revival of all time. The world will literally be revived and brought into unity under the sway of Papa's love and guidance. He will finally get His way and share His glory with us as we partner with Him. Papa wants it to be about all of us and not just Him. He has called us friends and friends are promoted together.

"Another touching vision that Papa showed me brought me to tears. I saw a totally black background and on top of this background were glowing tears. The tears were lit up and spread all over this black background. It was a beautiful sight and then suddenly, I realized that these were not just teardrops. The teardrops themselves were actually doors. I saw these supergiants walking through these doors with their heads raised high. They were confident and walking in intimacy with Papa. As I gazed on this wondrous vision, Papa spoke to me. He said, "Krista, every tear you've cried while you were suffering in bed this week represents **a warrior** that you will raise up. Those tears have not been in vain but have <u>birthed an army of supergiants</u> unlike the world has seen!"

"How exciting that <u>a new generation of supergiants is on the scene. I'm so ready to see them rise up together</u> and <u>form alliances of unity and love. They are leaders in their own right but they will know that they must come together</u> to make <u>a bigger difference.</u> This quality about them <u>shows their humbleness and wisdom</u>. Any strong leader knows that they don't have all the answers but <u>they also know that many strong leaders coming together can get the job done.</u> Are you ready to see and experience a revolution of Peace and Power? Supergiants have been birthed and toxicity has been purged out of this land. It's time to see a whole new world emerge with healing for all nations and tribes. I'm thrilled to be a part of something so wondrous and supernatural, aren't you? Krista, Kingdom Builders"//end

True unity and harmony are not humanly possible unless it's born of God, because our hearts are wickedly deceitful. True Unity requires a level of Love and Truth which can only come as we die to ourselves and are born of God's Spirit. T<u>here can be no wrong</u> <u>motives in our love - no mixture or selfishness, or impurity;</u> we can <u>not love others or act like we love them just to get something from them - whether it's to get our own needs met</u>. or to gain some advantage, or out of wanting to be seen or known. Our <u>hearts must</u> <u>be faithful to the Lord,</u>

our husband, and we must abide in His love for us so His love can flow to us and eventually through us. We **must not let someone else fill our need to be loved,** but we must save ourselves for the Lord and become fully satisfied in His love at all times

There is a process through which we learn to come out of hiding and to allow ourselves to be transparent before God and each other so that we can be pure. It involves confessing our sins to God and then even to one another at times as the Lord leads.

> *Confess therefore your sins one to another, and pray one for another, that ye may be healed.*
> *The supplication of a righteous man availeth much in its working.* (James 5:16, ASV)
>
> *Them that sin reprove in the sight of all, that the rest also may be in fear.* (1 Timothy 5:20, American Standard Version ASV)

Religion tells us that it is not appropriate to address sin openly, but sometimes the Lord wants us to do that because there can be great breakthrough and deliverance when we come out of hiding and out of our pride and fear. I have learned as much as possible to confess my shortcomings before my class so that it can be an example to them and it also keeps me open.

The cry of our heart must be wholly for Him to possess us, to become His habitation where we no longer live for ourselves nor let anyone or anything else be our source of satisfaction but for Him alone to be everything to us. But although we may agree to this singleness and desire it, we have no idea how many areas we need to be delivered from. He must reveal those areas to us as we cry out for Him so that we can repent and be forgiven and cleansed and take up our crosses and die to ourselves. Then we will have true love.

I've heard some horror stories of how some "apostolic fathers and mothers" have abused their sons and daughters, even using manipulation and controlling spirits to make them their own servants instead of building them and preparing them to become servants of the Lord. Sometimes they twist the truth of the Word into a lie to attract a following to themselves, or because they're insecure and feel threatened, or they're jealous, or afraid that they will be displaced. But the Lord has made a way for us to be healed of our insecurities, and if we do not take heed to God's warnings, the Word tells us there will be a more strict judgement against leaders who do these kinds of things. Leaders deserve honor, but they must be worthy of that honor by being obedient to the Lord themselves, setting examples and being faithful to the Lord in all their ways. It is only this kind of faithful father or mother that God will use to build His families.

God loves all of His people - whether a leader or a disciple, whether male or female, regardless of race or status, - and we must do all things as unto Him. He will hold us accountable for how we treat one another, and we will all be held responsible for being doers of His Word and not hearers only. He is not a respecter of persons - whether in blessing or in judgement.

Many church leaders have not learned to Fear God by attending to His Word, but the Lord will allow the storms and the fires to test every man's work and we will all know by that which remains standing, and by their fruit, what was of God or not. One of the most severe judgments of God is when He no longer shows you your sin but instead hands you over to your own deception.

> *If ye endure chastening, God dealeth with you as with sons; for what son is he whom the father chasteneth not?*
> (Hebrews 12:7, King James Version KJV)

The way to avoid being a bastard, is to stay open to the Word and to His true prophets who will speak the truth in love to you. -

> *"He who receives and welcomes you receives Me, and he who receives Me*

receives Him who sent Me. (Matthew 10:40, Amplified Bible AMP)

"Then I will come near you for judgment; I will be a swift witness against sorcerers, against adulterers, against perjurers, and against those who oppress the laborer in his wages and widows and the fatherless, and against those who turn away the alien [from his right], and those who do not fear Me [with awe-filled reverence]," says the Lord of hosts.

Then those who feared the Lord [with awe-filled reverence] spoke to one another; and the Lord paid attention and heard it, and a book of remembrance was written before Him of those who fear the Lord [with an attitude of reverence and respect] and who esteem His name.

"They will be Mine," says the Lord of hosts, *"on that day when I publicly recognize them and openly declare them to be My own possession [that is, My very special treasure]. And I will have compassion on them and spare them as a man spares his own son*

who serves him." (Malachi 3:5;16-17, Amplified Bible AMP)

To be a part of what God is doing in establishing His Families in His Apostolic House Churches, the Fathers and Mothers must walk in the fruit and character of Christ and not just by titles and man's appointments. They must be ordained by God.

Discipleship:

The Lord is <u>calling those who will train, equip and teach the young ones. To instruct them how to walk, how to war, how to resist temptation, how to recognize the tactics of the enemy and how to be sensitive to His voice.</u>

Discipleship has probably been my main ministry for around 40 years of my walk with God. For whatever reason, other Christians started coming to me for help when I still felt young in the Lord myself and was seeking God and pursuing Him with all my heart and strength. But I found that God had taught me things and that I was able to impart it to the hungry ones.

Eventually the Lord told me to lead prayer in the church. No one came for many weeks so I prayed alone, but finally a small group of loyal ones started attending. The Lord told me I was to lead them in worship, teach them God's word, and pray. We called the meetings "Warriors and Worshipers." It was during this time that the Lord revealed to me that I was teaching God's Ways. I didn't know that.

The subject of letting God kill your flesh makes a lot of people afraid, and the enemy attacks them in many ways, but for those who fought through we have a life-long bond and they are deeply grateful for their changed lives and how it has affected their families too. It has made them pure in their hearts and faithful to the Lord. One couple told me that their daughter reads my book over and over and also listens to me on Youtube repeatedly.

But there has also been a handful who have actually turned against me and started believing a lie, but the Lord has said that even though they turned away, that the seed of what they've been taught is still growing inside them and He said that the prodigals will return.

Prison Ministry

When the Lord told me He wanted me to do Prison Ministry, I didn't know what to expect because I had absolutely NO experience or knowledge with anything related to prisons. I never even met anyone who had ever been in prison. I didn't know if inmates would be able to relate to me, or me to them. And then it was a further surprise to me when the chaplains assigned me to work with the men because I didn't know if they would respect a woman minister. This was a real concern. In fact, one inmate asked to share after our meeting one day - and he said "When I was coming to the session today I looked and said 'Oh no, it's a woman.' Then when I got closer, I said 'Oh no it's an Asian woman.' He said when he saw me, he was expecting he would hear something dry and traditional, but then he said, "But Wow!" - - - so I was blessed to hear him as the Lord addressed my concerns and had touched their hearts.

I must acknowledge that I had an unusual experience in my 5 year Prison Ministry because even a couple of the deputies told me that they never saw anything like it in prison and they gave me their whole-hearted support and cooperation. I had nothing to compare it with so I didn't realize what a blessing this was at first.

At the start, I was ministering to a group of around 20 men, but because there was a precious pastoral inmate who had been ministering to them and making them hungry, and because the deputy could see the men were really responding to me, he told me I could come as early and as often and as long as I wanted.

The chaplain in charge got upset with me actually because she didn't like it that I was given such liberty. We were told to only stay 45 minutes, but that the deputies were in charge so they could change the time and we needed to obey them if we were asked to leave at any time. But no one ever thought the deputies would give anyone more than the 45 minutes. One chaplain finally came out to see what was going on, - and she said when she heard me preaching, she understood why the men responded like they did. I just pondered it in my heart what it all meant.

Eventually there were close to 100 men attending and I was speaking without a mic, but they never created a problem - they never talked or moved around, and the staff was amazed because they were all attentive and listening. After a few weeks, the inmates actually wrote me a love letter and said that when I came it was like Jesus Himself visiting them and they said that even the deputy loved me. There were so many testimonies of changed lives.

I knew it had to just be God, but it still surprised me. In fact MSNBC came out and televised interviews with the workers at the prison where I ministered. They were asking why this outpouring of God was taking place. They asked to interview me (but they never did). The inmates were really excited when MSNBC came because they wanted me to get some recognition, but I assured them it didn't matter. I was just grateful for what the Lord was doing. Not only were the inmates so blessed, but I was too. And now when I look back at this experience I realize it was His love and His spirit in me that made the difference. (Although this experience was such a rich and meaningful one, the Lord was not calling me to serve in this capacity after I moved because He had others things for me to do.)

It is written that the love of God is that we keep His commandments. When we walk in obedience to God - "leaning not to our own understanding" it will be a very pleasant lovely surprise to see all that is manifested in our lives because we were not seeking our <u>own glory, but His</u>. <u>He blesses us with restoring everything He</u> <u>required us to lay down,</u> but now we're fully satisfied and all things come to fulfillment - through Christ in us the hope of glory - and <u>not</u> <u>of ourselves</u> - so that we don't get lifted up in pride and self righteousness.

Marriage Counseling:

An important part of raising sons and daughters is giving them wisdom and counsel for their marriages, because marriages in the Kingdom are more significant than just being happy together.

Marriages serve a significant role in the Kingdom because they represent Christ and His Bride. Kingdom marriages are supposed to present a picture of a husband who knows how to love his wife as Christ loves the Church, and lay down his life for her, and a wife who genuinely can honor her husband and be his true helpmeet.

> *Husbands, love your wives, just as Christ also loved the church and gave Himself up for her, so that He might sanctify her, having cleansed her by*

*the washing of water with the word,
that He might present to Himself the
church in all her glory, having no spot
or wrinkle or any such thing; but that
she would be holy and blameless.
So husbands ought also to love their
own wives as their own bodies. He
who loves his own wife loves himself;
for no one ever hated his own flesh,
but nourishes and cherishes it, just as
Christ also does the church,
because we are members of His
body. FOR THIS REASON A MAN
SHALL LEAVE HIS FATHER
AND MOTHER AND SHALL
BE JOINED TO HIS WIFE, AND
THE TWO SHALL BECOME ONE
FLESH. This mystery is great; but I
am speaking with reference to Christ
and the church. (*Epi 5:25-32, NAS)

The Lord most often has me help couples simply by presenting the truth of His Word to them, speaking it to them in love. The specific parts I share and the timing of it, comes through the leading of His Spirit. He has shown me that the ONLY solution to any troubled marriage is whether they are willing to love the Lord by obeying His commandments and to seek the Lord so they can hear His voice and do what He tells them. When a couple is willing to do that, the victory is absolutely assured.

Once I see their hearts towards the Lord and one another, I don't need to know their whole history or their complaints against one another, I just let them know that the Lord led me into His victory in my own marriage and I share how He taught me to be washed in the Word, to pray it personally, to practice living it, and how He used my problems to kill my flesh, including my wounds, so that I was set free and became an overcomer. My own experience of living for decades in a painful marriage and how the Lord used it for my good so that I gained Christ - helps couples to believe me more.

The ways of God are so perfect - the success of our marriages isn't dependent upon our own strength or ability nor is it hindered by our wounds, our bad experiences, our lacks; - we just have to submit and obey to love and trust the Lord and He arranges all the old and present circumstances in our lives to work together for good. This means we will come to the end of ourselves and we will have His life in us and His ability to love, which will heal our lives and our marriages.

Chris and Danielle Anderson's Testimony

Chris and Danielle were originally married 14 years ago.

When they got married, they both came into the marriage with baggage from their past. Danielle had been in an abusive marriage for 12 years and had two small daughters. She had been raised in a Christian home with family issues leading to co-dependency and Chris was raised in a strong Catholic home with 7 siblings with similar family issues, leading to his feeling he never had a "voice" in his family. They both struggled with feeling loved and completely accepted by the Lord, even though they had a relationship with Him.

Their marriage started off roughly with trying to blend a family with trust issues on all sides. They knew they loved the Lord and wanted Him to be the center of their marriage, but they didn't know how to do that. They used the only "skills" they learned from their family of origin; consisting of "co-dependency, people pleasing, "skills" caused anger, frustration, lack of intimacy and disunity; all of which the devil used to separate them and drive them back to their co-dependent families. -

They began seeking out help through marriage counseling after only a year of marriage and many fights. The counseling only seemed to give them skills to try to communicate in a healthier way. It never dealt with the core issues, but nevertheless they tried years of counseling and spent thousands of dollars trying to get help. To no avail, the marriage limped along with both Chris and Danielle feeling frustrated as to how to make the marriage, they believed God brought together, even work. They were so desperate that they took a 7-month long class called Life Skills (3 times) which taught anger management skills, dealing with co-dependency, and healing from issues from their childhood. But even after gaining all of these tools and knowledge, their marriage would get better for only a short time and then the cycle of unhealthy behavior would start all over again.

They came to the point of separating for a few years while trying to work on their own issues in hopes of being able to come back together in a healthier relationship. The separation did help them see their own issues, but the communication and wounded self, brought out the anger and defensiveness. Danielle would draw back to her family and Chris would get frustrated and feel disrespected and not heard. This went on for years as the girls grew and got married and started having their own families. The youngest daughter and her husband and child were living with Chris and Danielle, trying to save money. The co-dependency in Danielle with her family kept a wedge of anger and disrespect towards Chris. She left Chris. She was deceived into thinking this was the only way to stop this unhealthy pattern they had in their relationship. She moved out with her daughter and son-in-law and grandchild. She filed for a divorce and went back to her family for support.

Chris was hurt and shocked over Danielle's taking the family and leaving him. The Devil had finally won it seemed. (Danielle had lost her faith that God could heal her marriage after all those years of trying to work on it on their own.) But Chris sought out another Christian community where he was loved on and taught about the Holy Spirit and His healing love. There, he met Dorothy, who gave him her book called, "It's Supposed to Kill You." It changed his life. He learned that he was loved completely by Christ and He didn't have to perform any longer to be loved. He also learned that to die to Self and Offensiveness would move him toward being single unto the Lord. He was truly filled with the Holy Spirit and God's love was flowing through him now. He had become a new creation in Christ.

This time of discovering God after the divorce from Danielle was probably the hardest yet most healing time in Chris's life, but God reunited Chris with his daughter that he was never allowed to be with since her birth 28 years ago and introduced him to his 9-year old grandson. -God never wastes anything. He uses all our mistakes and burnt ashes for good.

The two years that Chris and Danielle were divorced, God used it to bring healing and evaluation of His love to them both in their individual lives. They each individually never gave up hope and prayed that God would bring them back together and restore their marriage once and for all.

Chris's changed life overflowed and caught the attention of Danielle. She had never seen such a completely changed life before and wanted to learn what had happened. Chris started to share his testimony and how Dorothy and her book had helped change his life. At an all time low in Danielle's life, she was eager to read it and was hungry for what she saw in Chris. Chris and Danielle went to Dorothy's house for a counseling session for about 3 hours. It changed the direction of their lives. She counseled them to <u>seek the Lord FIRST and to LOVE HIM singly,</u> then Christ's love would flow in and through us and out to each other.

As Chris and Danielle began to put the Word into practice in their lives, God did it! He healed their individual lives and then restored their marriage as unto Him. - Chris and Danielle got remarried on July 1, 2017 by Dorothy Lee in a beautiful Spirit-led ceremony - 14 years after they had gotten married the first time. But now they were equipped with the knowledge of God's Ways to be able to continually walk in God's love and wisdom in every situation they would encounter.

"God is the only one who can restore the broken hearted and truly set the captives free. He truly did that for us and our family. We know without a doubt that NOTHING is impossible with God.

He brings beauty from ashes. Today, our heart is to share this Testimony."

Becoming Family:

Although I have belonged to an earthly family with parents, siblings, a husband and was a mother to 3 children, grandmother to 6, it's another thing to experience God's kind of "family" - which God is building around me lately. It's quite different to see yourself as the mother of a "family" with sons and daughters you've just met than having sons and daughters you've birthed.

When Mary and her sons asked to see Jesus, Jesus pointed to His disciples and said that they were His family because they were those doing the will of God. We **cannot be in God's family without sharing the total surrender of our lives to the will of God.**

It is that common bond of devotion and obedience to God that makes it possible. There can be no place for each one's own opinions nor can there be any suspicion or jealousy Instead there must be a mutual reverence for God. We must **all be "single" unto the Lord (or learning to be), being doers of the Word, being submitted one to another,** because there's no other ground for being unified. That's because it's only being devoted to the Lord that will impart grace to each member of the family to overcome the selfishness and neediness that prevents true love. And it is the apostles' doctrine that teaches us how to do that, as it was in the book of Acts. - A list of Do's and Don'ts won't work;

strategies and boundaries may help, but they are not able to produce relationships.

My heart is so overwhelmed at the quality and beauty of the people God has been adding to my life. I am experiencing the family God intended for me - as He intends for all His people to be part of their family. These relationships that God is developing around me are with people who have the fire of God's love first and foremost, but additionally, they actually see who I am and I can see who they are in God. It goes beyond the normal "teacher and student" interaction or of "mutual admiration", but it is actually developing into a real loving "mother and son/daughter" relationship of knowing one another in truth and watching over one another..as the Spirit is leading us in every encounter and situation.

The Lord told JoLynne Whitaker that He is about to <u>assign</u> <u>people to her life who will see her and **value her.** People who will **reciprocate her efforts and appreciate all she brings to the table, which is just about the same thing He has said to me.**</u>

He also said, to not be <u>investing in the wrong people or sowing</u> <u>into the wrong relationships</u>, -connections that were never even ordained by God. <u>The Lord said He is getting ready to send the ones</u> <u>who'll **appreciate and duplicate our commitment and authenticity**.</u>

At first when many were calling me "Mother/ Mom", I thought it was just a common, polite thing to do because I was an older woman. But starting in January last year (2017) when a man came up to me weeping and told me the Lord told him I was his mother,

I really started to pray about what that meant, for God to tell someone I didn't even know, that I was their mother. Then a few months later others expressed a desire for me to be their mom, and I began to recognize the significance and the sincerity of these requests. Since then, when the ones the Lord sends to me call me "Mom", I feel the honor in it and I feel a mother's love for them in return.

I believe this feeling of "family" denotes the maturing of the Body of Christ and God's timing. We are all becoming more "real" in our walk with God, and our relationship with one another is something God is building. It's a good feeling, like "real" families are being formed. I know this is what the Lord has intended His people to experience on earth, and it is happening. It's such a joy being with God's real sons and daughters and for them to genuinely consider me as their "mother".

Years ago I wondered about a prophetic words I received that I had a "family thing" about me, and I was like the "old woman who lived in a shoe and had so many children she didn't know what to do," but now I am beginning to understand and I am so grateful to be a part of this "heaven on earth" family. I can feel a real bonding in the Spirit, like <u>we really belong to one another and belong together.</u>

I feel so blessed because of the <u>purity of the love God has put</u> <u>in my heart for my true sons and daughters,</u> and because He has put that kind of love in them towards me also, yet there are no soul ties. We are not drawing together out of "neediness" or because we have something in common, or just that we like each other, or are lonely. This has b<u>een born from above and I feel His grace and</u> <u>blessing in it.</u> This has been a total surprise to me - to have a family of God's making. It is definitely a "heaven on earth" blessing. I already lived in a "heaven on earth" beautiful home God gave me, but now through this addition of his heavenly sons and daughters being joined to me, I am experiencing a depth of <u>blessedness beyond my ability to express,</u> and all in the love and purity of God.

We are recognizing it is His intention for us to need one another and yet keeping the Lord first. The Lord told me years ago that there will be no "joints supplying" in the Body unless we actually learn to submit to and receive into our hearts, one another's giftings. So even though I am a mother to sons and daughters, at the same time I am raising them up to be co-laborers, and I know how to receive anything the Lord gives them for me too. In fact when I received a word of adjustment from a "spiritual son" recently, it became a Key for me to bring a shift with one of my "natural sons".

I heard someone say recently that you have to "qualify" to have relationship, and I can see this is true. But for those who do qualify, by being single to the Lord, the Spirit is truly knitting us together as a family. Now I am not just discipling an individual but building that relationship with that individual to become a Family with Godly, mature relationships, where we have agreement in God and coming into one accord. I'm not uncomfortable anymore about being a Mother to those He sends me, because I now have God's heart to be that, and I can see His Kingdom further being established now.

Whether apostle or prophet, mother or disciple, son or daughter, we are ALL to be Bond slaves to our Lord. There is no hierarchy, but there is honor where honor is due, and we are ALL practicing, learning, honoring, and growing together to love one another as Christ loved us. There is **Godly discipline and structure without legalism or manipulation or controlling spirits** which have been all too prevalent in the Body of Christ, but still speaking the truth in love to one another. Our commitment is to the Lord, but as we all walk in the Fear of the Lord, there is honoring and esteeming of one another and actually submitting one to another, confessing our faults to one another - and speaking the truth in love, without hypocrisy, competition, envy or jealousy, and the fruit of the Spirit is the emphasis, not the gifts, even though they are necessary.

Chapter 8

Testimonies

The Lord told me He was sending a special person as a "Recompense" to me. Although I had to look up the definition of Recompense at the time, I recently read a greater revelation of what that means by a word written by prophet Phyllis Ford titled **"A Time of Recompense"**. (This is just an excerpt from that word.)

"We must come into the reality that when God recompenses, it is not like the world rendering payment upon a thing. Payment from the world's perspective is given with the understanding that the general deductions, taxes, and taxable amounts will apply and will affect the given amount.

"But when God says He will release His Recompense as a reward or payment concerning his promise. He is giving us based upon the amount owed, the time spent with interest, the grief and toil that accompanied the wait, the ridicule (embarrassment) that was endured when others whispered concerning our circumstance, the time during the lack thereof we endured, waited and even shared what you had with someone else just to make it through that particular season, and don't forget the time that you were just getting ready to get up and walk away and give up because of the pain of waiting.—-Add all that up and you have just barely touched upon what it meant when The Lord said He would take care of it. He meant He would pay, cover it, recompense. This is what the Lord meant when He said WAIT on it, it's coming. - It is the promise of something greater than that which was lost and was about to be received, and the promise brings with it payment that provides interest on what we think we lost. It gives back toil, sorrow and redeems with it TIME."/end

The promise comes and carries with it the reality of the Lord's will being worked out in our lives as we wait. It endures with understanding the process of our death while waiting on what He is about to do as He reveals it to us. We begin to **know who we really are, what we have become** and **how we will be** - now that it approaches manifestation.

As time has passed, I realize that He is sending many really special people to me as part of His Recompense in my life. Not only do I have the privilege of sharing my life with them, but I can see that they are uniquely qualified to be a blessing to me, to share their lives, their skills and their anointing with me.

Epi Moleli:

Epi is someone I've known many years. She told me her pride made her not want to return to my class when she found out that I was teaching on holiness and submission, but the Spirit pressed on her to keep coming. She was in my class one day when I was sharing my testimony of being married to my verbally abusive husband. Her job was to go home and translate the class from English to Samoan. But she told me that when she did that, that one day her husband Moi started crying and it went on for 2 weeks. I was so happy assuming that he must have been convicted and I always mentioned this testimony when I was teaching. However, after all these years have passed, I just found out a couple of years ago that her husband was not weeping in repentance, but weeping with gratitude because the teachings had changed Epi so much.

Epi told me she had been a very controlling, self-centered, rebellious, complaining kind of wife. She told me she was merciless towards him even though he was trying to work so hard and walking miles to and from work every day. When he got home she would just nag him about things. (It was very difficult for both of them to come to the U.S. without any connections or help, and not speaking English.) But the class convicted her - and Epi turned around and became an appreciative, caring and supportive wife and mother and a powerhouse warrior/intercessor.

The thing that made me laugh is that she shared her testimony in Samoa when she went for a visit 2 years ago, and she said that every woman in attendance was on her face in repentance.

Epi and Moi have been among two of my strongest supporters all these years, and God supernaturally healed Moi's meniscus which had been torn for 20 years, the first time he visited me up here in my new home.

Carl (not real name)

Carl was the first disciple the Lord sent me after I moved up to Meadow Vista. Through a very intricate process, the Lord conveyed to Carl that he was to contact me even though we hardly knew each other. It happened exactly like a word a prophet gave me saying that a special young man was going to contact me and that he would be a recompense in my life.

Carl had gone through a divorce and lost custody of his precious children as well as suffering extreme financial hardship. He felt the only thing he had left of his family was his pet dog. So even though Carl had to drive an hour and a half to come to my house, he chose to come 3 times a week and it was so special because he was so hungry and wanted to learn God's Ways.

I know he will prosper and have great success in the Kingdom because he is very devoted to obeying God and spending all of his after work hours being in His presence. His family recognizes the change in his life and are being affected by it. —At work he has also shared with me many testimonies of the ways the Lord has led him and protected him and given him grace and wisdom and strength.

Jacques Cook:

Very early on in meeting Jacques, he told me how his mother always wanted 2 things: to drive a minivan, and to make a recording with Jacques. Unfortunately she passed away before Jacques could help fulfill her desires, but I know this had a part in drawing us together because I was driving a minivan and had a deep desire to make a "home recording" with my son, who is the same age as Jacques and born the same month.

But as we started communicating, it brought us into a relationship that took us through 12 years of trials, testings, perseverance, sacrificing, patience, boldness, rebukes, trusting, submitting to one another. But the Lord blessed us with a covenant relationship that is very special because we endured so much, yet always spoke the truth to one another in love, and honored one another and were both faithful to obey the Lord. And I have come to realize that this is the kind of covenant love

<u>and unity that the Lord says will cause</u> <u>the World to know that we are His disciples.</u> This is what it looks like. He has brought us through that kind of experience.

I spent 6 days in his home last fall and it was living proof that all those years of testing had produced something special of His Kingdom. I could feel the depth of love and purity of Jacques' heart and it was like being in paradise.

<u>Jacques' Testimony</u>:

When I met apostle Dorothy Lee, I was on a ministry assignment in California. I saw her at one of the meetings. She was dressed very casual. She just looked like a short, little Chinese lady and was very unassuming. When I went to minister to her, the Holy Spirit said, "She's an apostle." I asked them to bring a chair up front and asked her to be seated. I told her that she'd be ushered into a new level of authority. The audience began laughing, because they knew I didn't know she was an apostle prior to releasing this word over her.

Afterwards, we remained in contact and developed a friendship. She was the first person to ever bring correction to me in love. She told me I had mixture in me, and that I was not where I thought I was yet. My first reaction was, "Who in the world does this little short woman think she is?" I thought, "She doesn't know me like that!"

However, she sweetly kept telling me that I need to check in this area, that I needed to do this, and that I needed to do that.

Next she gave me her book. When I read it, I began to see that she was living what she wrote about. As our relationship progressed, the thing that stood out was that I learned more from watching her life than I learned from what she said to me. Nothing I learned from her has been primarily from what she spoke. It has been the experience of her life and demonstration before my very eyes that taught me. This is what makes it easy to receive from her. I've been able to see God through her life.

As the relationship progressed more, we developed a place where we could trust the God in each other. The covenant doesn't mean that we mutually agree with everything. Yet, it would be stupid of me not to listen to somebody who has gone where I'm trying to go. She lived some things; and her wisdom lines up with the Word of God and shows validity with how she lived her life. As the relationship progressed even more I gained more respect for her. I gained a lot of momentum in my own life, by watching her, over the last 12 years we've been in covenant. She is a mother in Zion and a force to be reckoned with. It makes me happy to see her grow.

Even at the age she is, she's still growing. She keeps allowing God to pour into her.

The main thing I can take away from my relationship with her is that God is a progressive

God and if you stay with Him (like I've seen apostle Dorothy stay with Him), the benefits are beyond this world. I now believe all the goals you reach for are attainable, because her life has proven that.

Another thing I've gained from my mom is, "You are a fool when you reject wise counsel." Real love displays that when a person can correct you, they love you. She truly corrected me and wasn't afraid of me. Originally, I thought she was trying to insult me. Yet, she had God Himself backing her up and she wasn't afraid to correct me. I love her so much that I am determined to act on what I've learned and what she's imparted into my life, to make her happy. I found what makes her happy is when you obey God and get fulfilled in Him.

Todd Watson

Todd has only been with me since June 2017 so we haven't known each other for very long, but because he lives nearby at my Prayer House, he has spent a lot of time with me and done much to help me at my home. He has also spent a lot of time and great effort in helping me maintain and improve my Prayer House property, and I have been spending intentional time discipling him—-and often cooking for him, and I even cut his hair; so the Lord has developed a true mother/son relationship between us.

Much like Jacques, Todd shared his deep love for his mother with me and how he missed her because she died relatively young. But one day Todd said he was adopting me as his mom and I was quite surprised. I could tell he had been very prayerful about it before telling me and I knew he was sincere, so I felt honored, but was still praying about what this meant.

But the Lord began revealing to me the depth of relationship that He desires for His people to not only have with Him, but also with those He places in our lives. He wants us to walk together in His agape love and to become a part of His Family and be able to demonstrate this Family to the world, because by this shall all men know that we are His disciples, when we have love for one another.

Todd's testimony:

"I am 56 years old, graduated from college and had a 25 year career in insurance and financial management for which I attended many seminars and trainings, some taught by high-level, international speakers. But the trainings and teachings I receive from Dorothy, formally and informally, far surpass any training I've ever received in any capacity. Even though her style of teaching and discipling is very natural and it does not really feel like teaching is going on at all but just that I am gaining wisdom from a very wise person.

You can literally hear the Lord in the tone of her voice and in the power of her delivery as if He is speaking to me directly through her.

"The changes in my life since being taught by her are apparent to virtually everyone in my life, and these changes have affected the way I even see myself and are allowing me to see how the Lord sees me.

"I recently received these Images and reflections for Dorothy: "She is strong, prophetic, wise, gifted, full of Love and her heart is to share His teachings and desires for us. She is so sweet in her nature and methods - it feels more like I'm talking to a loved one than to a world-class educator. It's very exciting to see how her reputation for mentoring, counseling, living and teaching in God's true gifting has increased. She just overall is a guide to those with a hunger for growth in the Lord.

"God is showing me..."And so the next chapter of Mom's life begins - the rapid ascent of Dorothy Lee from grass roots apostle and locally known spiritual powerhouse to national and international keynote speaker and advisor to the world's foremost business, religious and political leaders. Accompanied by a close team she refers to simply as her "spiritual children" this team of powerhouse speakers and leaders are touching all levels of society and are impacting entire regions and all generations. This is creating the greatest revival of spirituality and faith in God the world has ever known.

"Asked how this Is so impacting, the team universally reply, 'Mom has shown us how through death of our flesh, we become one with God. His timing is our timing, His ways are our ways, and His ways are perfect!.'"

Kimberly Wallace's Testimony:

I was asked by a friend of mine, to check out this class that Dorothy Lee was teaching.

Dorothy always seemed to be in the presence of God whenever I saw her worshipping. Other than that, I only knew her superficially, as an older woman, who regularly attended the Marvel Upper Room.

It was a Saturday morning, and my roommate agreed to meet me at the class. I arrived and there was a nice-sized group gathering. I have to be honest, as Dorothy began teaching the class, there was nothing particularly mesmerizing, enigmatic or charismatic about her teaching. As a matter of fact, I thought she was outdated, using black and white pictures and not utilizing any form of Powerpoint slide presentations! I remember thinking to myself, this might be a long class...

I set up my tablet and my little pad of paper, so that I could scribble down some ideas, as I was taking notes. As I listened to her speak, I thought, Oh I need to share with her the Redemptive Gifts, Leadership Workshop and Spiritual Warfare teachings, that I do internationally.

I was quite busy writing down all these notes and things I wanted to share with Dorothy. Suddenly I heard God's loud voice as though he was yelling and standing right there in front of me, **"Stop it Kimberly!** Stop with your busyness and thinking about what you can do for her. I have put much inside of her. There is an impartation that can only be received while sitting in the presence of my Holy Spirit and listening to her voice. You are here for an impartation! —-**Receive it!"**

I was completely stunned! In fact, I was so shocked that I told Dorothy about that experience I had just had with the Holy Spirit! After which, I listened intently, and stopped taking notes!

Because of that class, I had been invited into a personal relationship by the Holy Spirit with Dorothy.

Some time later, the very day I returned from Australia, in March 2017, my mother had passed away. It was a very difficult time for me. A month had passed after my mother's death, when I went up to Dorothy's. After helping her on the computer in her office, I bent over to give her a hug goodbye. As I did, I burst into tears. Oh my goodness, I thought; That sure felt a lot like hugging my mother. I shared this with Dorothy.

From that time on, I began to treat her and feel like, she was a mom to me. Dorothy walks in a peaceful calm that only God could have given her and has a generous mothering heart. I have learned so much about the goodness of God by being around her and growing a deep personal relationship with her. She is truly my mom!

Nancy Crites' Testimony:

I moved to the East Bay in 1992. My family and I had had some hard times, my husband had been laid off of his great job in Texas and we had had a year of searching for work. I was a stay-at-home mom at that time of my life, and the move and long stint without work for my husband had taken a toll on the entire family. I had chosen to attend Shiloh Christian Fellowship in Oakland, even though it was over 40 minutes by car from my home, because I was looking for MORE. I enjoyed the worship there, and the teaching, but I kept asking myself over and over again why I was there. What was the LORD's purpose for me in this very strange new part of the world?

After 18 months of attending Shiloh, I read in a flyer that there was prayer every day in the Fireside room. I decided to check it out, and on that day, my entire life changed! I met Dorothy Lee and she began to teach me about God's ways, and His Character and my life exploded into the fruit of the Spirit in a very short time. I began to learn about obedience, and about God's personal character and how I had to "take up my personal Cross daily" and live for HIM in the LOVE that is Jesus. Dorothy helped me to see my selfishness and to recognize how to love others with the LOVE of God. This changed my life. I began to rejoice in all things, I could accept criticism without breaking down as I had before, I could forgive on a whole new level. Very quickly, Dorothy became my friend and I began to understand the KINGDOM of God on a whole new level. I felt privileged, chosen and loved.

My husband was not a believer and was even hostile to my Christian faith, but Dorothy showed me how to love him and serve him in a new way. This resulted in good fruit in my home, and in my personal life, and in my relationship to my then small children. I would get up every morning and run around like crazy getting the children off to school and making sure everything was clean and tidy so that I could jump in the car and make it to the Fireside Room by 10 am when prayer started. We prayed every day, and I would rush home around 2:30 to greet the children and prepare dinner for my husband. It was a wild time! I learned so much, and began to understand the deeper things of the Kingdom.

Of my three children, I have one daughter Caroline, who has spent a great deal of time with me in her adulthood. She was so moved by the testimony and fruit of what the ministry of Dorothy Lee had done for me that she recently wrote Dorothy a letter telling her how thankful she was for her influence in my life, as she had gained so much from those second-hand teachings herself!

So as you see, Dorothy's anointing stretches over generations! What a blessing that is!

Now it is 2018, and I have not been able to pray with Dorothy on a regular basis since 1995. We moved to Southern California then, and from there were called to Germany. Those times of prayer with Dorothy still sustain me, and our friendship has lasted these many years. Dorothy has a special gift from the Holy Spirit of Wisdom. Her wisdom has helped me many times to understand God's Ways and substitute them for my own, both in times of crisis and in times of blessing. The way is indeed narrow, but with someone like Dorothy and the precious LORD on your side, you can make it. Dorothy's teachings are rich and powerful. You are in for a treat as she leads you to a greater understanding of the LORD's ways, so that we can die to self and live to Him! The Kingdom of God is our goal and we are his people! As you read this book, I welcome you to the great adventures that await you as you go deeper into the discovery of God's ways! Nancy Crites, Hannover, Germany

Pastora Jina Embuscado's Testimony (JTR Ministry HK)

"We miss you and I miss you personally. How can we forget your message and testimony of "dying to self"? That was our preparation for climbing the Mountain of the Lord. We were being prepared for the journey from glory to glory, and the rest is history .... a glorious walk with God by His Spirit, with cleansing from within, being changed and being transformed person-ally ...and cleansing the church too.) As you had said to me .. (I didn't forget ... because it was such a relief to me) ... "Pray for them, love them but let them go if they want to go" ... I learned that from you and I don't have pain anymore when those who don't want to obey God go out of the church. Thank God for the comfort...

"That was one of the more important things and the purpose for why you were sent to me ... to bring me encouragement...

Do you remember the time you were here when some of our leaders went out of the church and I was being bullied by the enemy that I was nothing? .... that I did nothing good because people left the church? ... I was demoralized. But then suddenly ... before you preached you said... "Pastora Jina you are doing a great job here for His glory and in the lives of these ladies."

And I know that at that time .... that was the very perfect message i needed to hear from the Father through you that lifted me up... thank you so much, Mom Dorothy.

I'm very happy when you remember me and send prophetic messages to me. It helps me a lot. - I just came back from a mission trip in the Philippines with Pastora Amy. It was a very wonderful trip. We visited at least 4 places of JTR ministries pastored by women of God who were all trained here in

HongKong and now walking in their calling. They are really paying the price, but joyfully serving the Lord, standing firm and moving forward.

Apostleship -

I so appreciate how God speaks to us through His prophets as their words are such a good way for me to check on myself.

One prophet wrote, that Apostles have been commissioned by the Father Himself to uncover and <u>reveal Jesus Christ as the</u> <u>foundation, the</u> <u>cornerstone, and head of the Church. True apostles</u> <u>consistently teach, preach, and prophesy on the life,</u> <u>death, burial, resurrection, ascension, and second</u> <u>coming of Jesus Christ. If HE Himself is not their</u> <u>central focus and message, they are NOT legitimate</u> <u>apostles.</u>" —(According to this word, I'm thankful to see that I'm a legitimate apostle!)

In 1 Thessalonians 2:5-12, Paul writes concerning five specific earmarks of apostolic ministry. They are as follows:

Apostles do not lord their authority over the saints, but rather <u>they minister in gentleness as a</u> <u>nursing mother </u>tenderly cares for her own children.

<u>Apostles are full of fond-affection for the saints</u> <u>and impart life</u> <u>and love through relationship, </u>not networking or hierarchy.

Apostles are <u>not greedy and do not desire to be</u> <u>a financial</u> <u>burden </u>to those to whom they minister.

Apostles are fathers who <u>exhort, encourage, and challenge the</u> <u>saints to walk in a manner worthy of God's call</u> on their life.

Apostles do not come to flatter saints with their words nor do they seek glory and praise from men.

<u>True apostolic fathers who, through love and care, will properly</u> <u>impart both their own lives and revelation of Jesus Christ, and raise</u> <u>up and release genuine sons and daughters." //end</u>

Prophets have told me that I would be writing about what the apostolic ministry really should be about, and they also told me I am an apostle to apostles, a general to generals, a leader to leaders, and that I would be restoring a True Foundation to the church.

As I've read the above prophecies and more, I don't really feel like I "know more" than any of them, and that I can learn more from them actually, but the only thing that might be different is that the Lord brought me to the "death of myself", and I believe I've been able to see things differently than the majority of Christians because of this experience, and that I can impart revelation in a unique way as God intends.

I have been given a plumb-line revelation of how to walk in God's ways and although the Lord is still teaching me things, I am experiencing rich Kingdom results and breakthroughs in my life and ministry and this is the foundation He wants me to restore in the church and in apostolic ministry in particular.

There are varying apostolic functions with many different streams and emphases.My intention is not trying to define these, but rather my intention is to restore the foundation of sound doctrine that will cause the Body of Christ to grow to the full stature of Christ and edifying the Body through taking His yoke of meekness and lowliness upon us as we serve them. My ministry is to model and impart my revelation and not just teach it.

1 Cor 12:28 says that God has appointed in the church <u>first of</u> <u>all apostles,</u>...Many have taken this to mean first in being honored and first in the line of authority, but from what the Lord has taught me, my experience is that to be "first" as an apostle should be -"first" to submit and obey the Lord to take up our cross and die; the first to keep His commandments to forgive, to show mercy, to be patient and kind, to be long suffering; the first to love, and be filled with joy and peace. - In other words, we should be first to be partakers of His holiness which is to have the nature and character of Christ with all the fruits of the Spirit worked into us, and then first to be Doers of His Word in every situation, and in all relationships (not waiting for others to submit to us only); living in purity, in humility, in truth, in rest and sometimes in boldness, the Lion and the Lamb freely manifesting as it pleases Him.

And to the degree we have submitted unto death, and it's now Christ living in us, we will be yielded to Him to speak or move through us as

He wills. We will overcome all things - including offense, because in our dying, "Self" is no longer on the throne of our lives. and instead Peace rules our spirit, and we know how to let Peace act as referee in all things and to be led by it. Our dying produces in us a place for the King to be enthroned and reigning, and it prepares us to let Him do it in and through us. The Lord told someone recently -"I don't just want you to Decrease so I can Increase, but you need to Disappear so that I can Appear".

Apostles should love His appearing as they are disappearing.

There is the Broad way which leads to destruction, and there is the Narrow way which leads to LIFE. If we don't choose to be one of the fewer who walk in the Narrow way of the Cross, we automatically will be walking in the Broad way of just doing what seems good or right in our own eyes, walking according to our own understanding. We need to know that the Word says "My people perish for a lack of knowledge." In other words, Ignorance is not an excuse. The prophets are blowing the trumpets and warning the Church loud and clear - This is the Way of the Lord - Walk in it!

Be holy as He is holy! (Those who are pretenders will be attacking and falsely accusing those who choose to obey God, those who speak Truth, in order to cover up their own rebellion and stubbornness and lack of love.)

> *"He gave some apostles ....for the equipping of the saints for the work of service, to the building up of the body of Christ."*
>
> (see Ephesians 4:7-16)

The Bible says the "Letter kills and the Spirit gives life." If we just try to do our ministry by following the letter of the law or even following a God-given vision, with our senses, it won't work because of the sin nature of man. However, since we know we are called to equip the saints for the work of service and to build up the Body of Christ, if we have died and Christ is now living in us, our ministry of equipping and building will be pure and effectual because He will be the source of everything needed - whether wisdom, grace, strength, love or provision, -and nothing we will do in this regard will be tainted with selfishness, lusts, greed, pride - all of which caused the downfall of many of the great healing evangelists. But the Lord has said He would **never again pour out such power on a "man" without Holiness" because of all the corruption** that evolved.

True apostles will be holy as He is holy and impart it to their disciples through not only teaching, but by example of how they live. They will live by every Word that proceeds forth out of the mouth of God. They will live by the faith of the Son of God, leaning on the Lord who is become their Beloved, their life, and His strength has been made perfect in their weakness. They will be protected and led by the Peace of God, bringing them into His Rest. They will share the Joy that was set before Jesus as He endured the suffering and they willingly fulfill His sufferings that others may be saved. They will lay down their lives for others because there is no greater love, and this sometimes includes giving financial support even to their disciples as needs may arise. (see James 2:14-20) And they will be continuously filled with His love as their hearts are always worshiping with gratitude and thanksgiving for their Savior Jesus Christ.

In a prophetic <u>excerpt by Jeremiah Johnson, he saw in a vision, **true apostles and prophets restoring the foundation of** the Church and many of them were teaching other young people how to properly lay the foundation. God is raising up a remnant in the American Church that will be **sound in doctrine, embracing the gospel of self-denial, and they will not walk in fear, anger, violence, and depression.**</u>

Glenn Jackson's word: "The chief desire of the holy apostles and prophets concerning God's children is **to lead them into the place [the "inner chamber"] wherein they [those who will "hear"] are both developing and maintaining an absolute trust in the Father and His Word**. - <u>You are raising up a true, working five-fold ministry </u>throughout the

remnant Church - <u>righteous, delegated authorities
whose first and foremost heart-desire is to help</u> **lead
Your people into the perfect intimacy with You** -—
The only way that My children can continually
"rise above" the <u>schemes of the Evil One is to be
found "abiding" in Love.</u>

"<u>Being an apostle is a function, not a position
of en-titlement, even though the Lord wants His
leaders esteemed because of their sacrifice and
obedience and the wisdom they</u> have. But He wants
us to give honor to whom honor is due, regardless
of function." // end

<u>Jennifer LeClaire was given a word about</u> new
<u>kingdom reformers, kingdom expositors, Apostolic
lawmakers</u> - all burning with a **holy fire,** and
they'll **know the depths of God** having tasted **and
known Him, and they** will both <u>live and teach</u>
from the position of **"abiding" in the fullness** of
their **Covenant-relationship** with God - Angels will
be working **with the new Apostolic Reformers,** to
reshape & reform the earth with truth. Truth will
grow brighter, the ways of God will become more
apparent for man to walk in the lamp of God's
word.

<u>R</u>eformation will **reach every government,
every king, and monarch on the earth.** The sword
of truth will reign and **bring kingdom truth and
prosperity, kingdom health and healing, kingdom
restoration, and kingdom righteousness**. But the
kings must **humble themselves to these ways being**

<u>revealed</u> in <u>our times, they must embrace the new</u> <u>so they can receive the new wine, the new oil, the</u> <u>new dispensation of Christ's own kingship</u> in their domains!"

"<u>The primary calling of ALL true apostles is to</u> <u>unveil the glorious person of Jesus Christ to His</u> <u>body. (Col 1:17; Eph. 3:8-11)</u>

Women in Apostolic Ministry

This is an hour and day when the Lord is significantly raising up women in leadership. It took me many years of receiving prophetic words about my being an apostle before I finally believed it. But now the prophetic words are confirming in every way all the words spoken to me all these years, and not only to me, but to all women who have walked through trials in trust, intimacy and obedience to the Lord.

Also many books have been written about women leaders in the Bible, and as I've studied them, I have found them to be accurate accounts and that it is clear that God is not against women leaders. These books also explain about the Bible verses that seem to forbid women from speaking in church or teaching a man and how they had these requirements because of the culture in which they were living, and as I've prayed, I know this is true.

However, one verse continued to trouble me and it is always quoted in regards to women in ministry-

> *There is [now no distinction in regard to salvation] neither Jew nor Greek, there is neither slave nor free, there is neither male nor female; for you [who believe] are all one in Christ Jesus [no one can claim a spiritual superiority].*
> (Galatians 3:28, AMP)

I had reservations about using this verse presumptuously since the Lord took me through such an arduous path of preparation and taught me some things that didn't line up. The biggest question I had was about 1Tim 2:14-15

> *And Adam was not deceived but the woman, having been completely deceived, has come to be in transgression.*
> *But she will be saved by The Childbearing, if they continue in faith and love and holiness with sound-mindedness.* (1 Timothy 2:14-15, Disciples' Literal New Testament)

I thought "this is not a mistranslation as some of the verses about women proved to be" - so I sought the Lord with my whole heart so I could understand.

What He showed me was quite a surprise. He said that the "Childbearing" pertained to a woman giving birth— but it was to **birth Christ in us as we've submitted and trusted God in the**

trials He took us through. - Now it made sense, because as we fully submit to the Lord and obey His commands, He is killing our flesh and setting us free from the "natural DNA" of a woman and free from the curse she was under. We become new creatures in Christ and have His DNA as Christ (the Word) is formed in us and birthed through us.

The subject of whether Women can be Apostles is still debated to this day, but the Lord has uniquely prepared me for this role as He took me through 48 years in the wilderness to teach me that "Yes, it can be done by a woman and like a woman," I can now confidently share my revelation with the Body of Christ because He has tested and proven His Word in my life. (In my prison ministry, the Lord told a pastor, "Did you every think I could look so good in a woman?)

Patricia King shared: Women of God Arise! You are "Life givers"

The Lord said to Patricia that He has anointed and appointed women to create life and impart life in everything that we do and wherever we go. Everyone and everything can receive the Lord's life because we are His Life-givers and releasers of Life.

In this season, those dreams that seemed to have died will arise with the breath of His resurrection life. We will speak to dry bones, birth God-given mandates and they will come to life because we carry the breath of God's Spirit... His love.

Women of God will rise up in the nations in this hour and do exploits that touch every sphere of society. They will proclaim God's **Life-producing gospel and** will arise to **give voice to God's wisdom, power, and purposes."** - Many women even in their latter years will give birth to significant Kingdom ministries.

Out of the place of intimacy with God, women will be impregnated with all we were created for.

By apostle Axel Sippach

"For 700+ years **Junia** was the lost first "WOMAN" apostle. According to Paul, she, along with her husband, was an OUTSTANDING apostle.

Traditionally they were said to powerfully preach in pagan areas seeing pagan temples closed and new churches built on those sites. - She was a GAME CHANGER.

In this present apostolic reformation, prepared women are now receiving the respect and recognition many deserve.They are being raised up in 5-fold ministry positions, including APOSTLES . - So it is time for the church to get free from religious thinking and to JUST GET OVER the bias against women as apostles.

In my first book "It's Supposed to Kill You" I have shared the pain and the long-suffering it took for God to "kill" me (my ego, my will, my ways) so that He could sit on the throne of my life. As I obeyed the Lord and kept my eye singled to Him, I learned these lessons:

1. We need to submit and obey the Lord as He leads - so there will be no more rebellion in us, and so we can see the reverse of the curse on us. The Lord revealed to me after years of obedience, that every act of submission is building Christ's true authority in our lives, building His throne in us.

When I told God I wanted to do His will and be pleasing to Him, The only thing the Lord told me was that He had given me a husband that was perfect for me and He wanted me to submit fully to him. It took me practicing to obey the Lord through many tears, much repentance, and continual forgiveness and faith before I was able to genuinely surrender my will. He wanted me to give Him all my pain and my many great fears, and I had to lay down all my own needs and desires, as He kept enabling me to believe for His promises, but He gave me His grace to endure. And He gave me His Truths to guide me to my freedom, and I had His life in me to make it.

2. Through much prayer and obedience, we are saved by giving birth (1Timothy 2:15)

I obeyed God to submit to my husband, being a doer of the Word for over 30 years! I could definitely see the change taking place in my life as the years rolled by, but it also took prayer and seeking God for understanding about women apostles and why it was all right with Him when the Word seemed to indicate the opposite.

Finally one day He revealed to me that the phrase "saved by giving birth" meant that we could give birth to Christ in us as we obey His commands. He is the Word made flesh, so as we obey His Word, His Word becomes flesh in our lives too. So that's why we're no longer the "female" whom Paul would not allow to teach a man, but we can become new creatures in Christ and we are no longer living with the DNA of a Woman and under her curse, but we have been set free by the Blood of the Lamb and have His DNA.

3. We can't just claim the promises of God as being ours without the corresponding obedience and fruit being manifested. In my case, He enabled me to love my husband as I ought.

I lived in 1Peter 3:1 for years, reading and praying through it, word by word, over and over, in order to be sure I knew the Lord's will and to put it into practice, because honestly it seemed impossible to be this kind of wife, especially when I would read that Sara called Abraham "lord", it made me cringe. But miraculously it happened to me one day by God's grace. He enabled me to humble myself that much!

> *Likewise, ye wives, be in subjection to your own husbands; that, <u>if any obey not the word</u>, they also may <u>without</u>*

<u>the word</u> be won by the <u>conversation</u> <u>of the wives;</u>
While they behold your chaste conversation coupled with fear.
Whose adorning let it not be that outward adorning of plaiting the hair, and of wearing of gold, or of putting on of apparel;
But let it be the <u>hidden man of the</u> <u>heart, in that which is not corruptible,</u> <u>even the ornament of a meek and</u> <u>quiet spirit,</u> which is in the sight of God of great price.
For after this manner in the old time the holy women also, who trusted in God, adorned themselves, being in subjection unto their own husbands:
<u>Even as Sara obeyed Abraham,</u> <u>calling</u> <u>him lord:</u> whose daughters ye are, as long as ye do well, and are not afraid with any amazement. (1 Peter 3:1-6, KJV)

4. We can have differing opinions as to interpretations and translations of the Word, but when it comes to Fruit, there's no argument anymore. The Word says we will be known by our fruits. (see Matthew 7:16 and Gal 5:22-23) The fruit of the Spirit is love, joy, peace, forbearance, kindness, goodness, faithfulness, gentleness and self-control. Against such things there is no law.,

and they should all be manifesting in our lives appropriately - not only on the outside to others, even to our enemies, but inwardly in our heart attitudes also, because out of the abundance of the heart, our mouths will speak.) He is meek and lowly, and we are supposed to take His yoke upon us and learn of Him so that we can look like Him.

Deborah:

A prophet shared that the Lord is raising up women now who KNOW HIM; modern day Esther's, Deborah's, and Mary's to stand with PASSION and CONVICTION on their platform of influence. He said the Lord is awakening women and MAKING their voice LOUD to bring CHANGE, LIFE, to stand for RIGHTEOUSNESS and to see incredible visitations of His Glory.

God has called me to be a part of the end time, prophet/judge Deborah company. In studying in depth about her, I have learned many of her traits and can recognize that many of them have been operating in my life. In particular she was known to have **wisdom and discernment** and had an **Overcomers' anointing** and was a **Mother in Israel**, all of which I am walking in to some measure.

Deborah's are not Jezebel's so there will be no manipulation nor selfish ambition. The fact that **Barak trusted her** so completely I'm sure was due to the fact of her sanctification. She must have had favor with him because he could discern her heart and spirit, since **true authority** is always a product of a heart that is in **total submission** to the Lord. *(The Lord showed me that all my submission to Him had established His throne in my life.)*

I remember the day in the early 2000's when the Lord told me "Now that you don't have anymore rebellion - (I walked in total submission to my husband for the first 35 years of my life with God) "NOW, do not let your husband (or anyone) intimidate you anymore." There was nothing left in me to accomplish that, I had been so broken, but because of knowing God's ways, I took it as just the next step of obedience in faith for me.

Over time, I learned that through those many years of submission to God's commands, my heart was healed and my attitude towards my husband and other men was one of true respect and honor, and I've come to realize that even when I ministered to the many men in my Prison Ministry, that they could feel this honor also and the love I had for them, and they responded wholly to me - even to their own and my own surprise and the surprise of the deputies and chaplains.

Like Deborah, God has put a cry in my heart **to deliver His people from the bondage that idolatry and sin have caused,**-

He has given me a heart for **righteousness, justice and mercy.. that will produce the moral purification of His people and the nation,** -and like Deborah, my life has been lived "**with a psalm on**

my lips and a sword in my hand", or sometimes a surgeon's scalpel. I want God's people delivered for their own blessing and to bring glory to the Lord

With purity comes the ability to see God in all things, and also to see God's purity in His wisdom and love for us. Only in this purity can one be used as a "judge" for His purposes, because without purity, we will be in darkness and not be able to see accurately, much less judge accurately. We will have a mixture that will cause us to move in error and be deceived. *(Many times I've been accused of things but when I asked the Lord, Why does this keep happening? - He told me that they accuse me of things that are in their own hearts. They assume you are like them.)*

Wake Up Deborah and Arise! by Susan Vercelli 4/ 2/ 17

"The Lord is awakening, bringing forth, and raising up, His Deborah's! - Mother of Israel arise and shine for your light has come and the glory of the Lord rises upon you!

"There is a fresh release..There is an awakening happening in the spirit of the Lord, there is a new movement coming, and we will see the Mothers arise..we will see the rise of the prophet, and the judge! -we will see the rise of the Deborah company of the Lord! (see Judges 5)

"This Deborah is going to birth new life into God's Israel .

I arose..As a mother to Israel!
My heart is for the princes of Israel!
The willing volunteers among the people! Praise the Lord!
This Deborah anointing is an equipping oil for the princes!
Training and equipping for battle!
The Deborah's will bring the oil to the willing volunteers for the preparation of the army of the Lord. .
This Deborah is a type of spiritual Mother.. who will build up and supply the soldiers!
This Deborah will lead as the eye of the body, and have prophetic vision, strategy, intercession, divine direction for the battle, -to empower, equip others, help others to overcome! And help them through the battle!
This Deborah will bring a restoration to the Sons of God even as a mother would guide and nurture her sons, and activate, and revive them. Her prophetic word of the Lord will bring new life to the princes of Israel!
This Deborah will be fierce in battle and as a protector, this warrior bride will issue the command of God for the destruction of the enemy. .
This Deborah will lead and equip, aid and help the Barak leadership in the

army of God in the kingdom of God."
/end.

The Market Place:

Giving Wisdom to Businessmen and other leaders:

In the late 70's I received this word from a company of prophets: "I'll lift you up and stand you in business circles, amongst business persons; to give wisdom, deposit and understanding of business venture and realms; You'll make a mark among men desperately seeking for a word of counsel, for their salvation and prosperity.. Man will usher you in and will ask of the counsel and advice of the ability to detail things. You will share on how to live in Peace and wisdom. They will be blessed by your faithfulness unto Me. You'll have doorways where you can speak with authority and power.

"You are My Spokeswoman -you will stand in the professional arena, with those in authority, and expertise, but you'll have something to say like apples of gold - and with a silver tongue and I will cause words and understanding."

"**Men of Wealth will come and seek your favor** because you **have Words of Life that change hearts; you cut through man's teachings and thinking and give the real Peace; they'll seek your favor, your blessing, and your teaching.**"

"**Do not try to force things to happen.** Let Me do the leading, and set the pace. I will open doors for you, and align you with the right people that will be assigned to you as you fulfill your destiny purpose in Me. It is My doing. I will lead you and guide you continually, and set things in order for you. **You will be prepared** for every good work **that I assign and commission you to do,** and I will go before you and <u>prepare the way.</u>

"<u>**I will prepare the people, places, and things**</u>, for nothing is outside of My authority and control. My purposes shall unfold, and you will grow into your destiny, without failure, as I mature you,"

The Lord has also told me that I would bring reconciliation and healing to nations, as well as stand before kings, that He would bring leaders to me on the level of Billy Graham and Oral Roberts, and much, much more. - We are told that we should do warfare with our prophetic words and to stir them up, but I humbly have to say that the Lord has told me SO MUCH, that it overwhelms me to even think about it, because it makes me feel sick - like the feeling of eating too many cream puffs for dessert.

The Word says that righteousness is profitable for all things, and this definitely includes success in businesses, in government and every sphere of life. And because Jesus is made Wisdom and Revelation unto me, I have the very source of wisdom living in me to be able to share His wisdom, and I know that it is not of myself, but walking in His ways of the

Cross has positioned me with great authority as it will for anyone who is willing to pay the price.

One of the things that can block a Christian's progress is when they don't understand what "righteousness" means. In the simplest form, it means to Believe God and have FAITH which is counted as righteousness unto us, as it was said of Abraham who believed God. (see Rom 4:3) When we have true Faith, it will cause us to obey His voice regardless of pressures from others or from our own fears. And when we are fully obeying God to trust Him in all things, all of our acts will eventually be with pure motives in our heart, because the Lord will take us through the fire to purify us..

The interesting thing is that now in the beginning of 2018, I can see a significant inroad to the fulfillment of this word about my being in the business environment. The Lord is just setting it all up - the right people, the right timing, the right setting. - It's all coming into line with His prophecies to me....including one written just recently that said, "This is what she was made for. She has been shunned by religious and conformist folks - but she is prepared."

David Del Dotto, VP of Sales & Operations: "Dorothy has so much to give to whom the Lord sends that is open. She is not religious, she is real.— I was a frustrated karate kid and Dorothy was my Miyagi tuning me for the match."

Thank you Lord that you took all these years to prepare me so that I can be a faithful servant to fulfill your will. My trust is in you, and I know that no one who trusts in you will be disappointed or ashamed and that you will do abundantly above and beyond all I could ever ask or even imagine.

Building House Churches:

It was a shock to me to read the word (below) about Apostolic House Churches, because it described exactly the things the Lord has given me to do. I was told, "You know things you don't know that you know." - and I'm discovering that to be true more and more. As I listen to other apostolic and prophetic ministers, it causes me to more fully understand the significance of what He has taught me.

Apostolic House Church..by Susan Vercelli Feb 2018

"What I see and hear the Lord say..Is that the Lord is positioning, planting, moving his apostles into houses chosen for the glory of the Lord. (*The Lord did this for me in 2014 when I moved into the home He chose for me, which I now call "Eagles' Retreat".*)

We are going to see an increase of apostolic house churches..

The glory of the Lord will invade these houses.. (*Several prophets have come to my home and given visions of His glory here.*) There will be apostles planted in the cities chosen by God and they will **equip disciples from these houses.** (*I do this equipping 2 or 3 times weekly.*) There are going to be **family relationships, - family suppers too,** as the Lord will build <u>real family relationship in</u> <u>His house.</u>.(*This is exactly what the Lord has done here. I have real sons and they lovingly call me their mom., and we watch out for one another.*) "Jesus did house church..He stayed at different people's houses and the whole house got saved.

"As Jesus wasn't mantled in the local religious organizations of His day, neither were the first apostles. (*And neither was I.*)

They were sent..to the synagogues or religious systems of men to testify..-yet they weren't received by the false religious institutions of men. .So as in the day we are in..Because the modern day lukewarm status quo church systems of men are so corrupt and full of mixture and the glory is not dwelling in them. (*I was removed from 2 churches even though I was faithfully committed for 26 years in one and over 10 years in the other - always laboring in love and in prayer and in teaching God's ways.*)

"The Lord shows me **that as He is setting up apostolic house churches..**there's a movement of God for buying houses for those who are apostolic/

prophetic and chosen for this ministry of House Churches in the chosen cities where God has placed them..

"And the Lord is releasing funding - <u>financial blessings for</u> <u>these chosen- to purchase homes</u> so they can be the owners of these house churches.. They will operate in the glory of the Lord.. (*The Lord has repeatedly told me that many would pour finances into my ministry as they see the purity and wisdom God has given me.*)

"I see many open up their homes for the glory of the Lord...like the inn used by the good Samaritan.. These homes will be like the inn. and the ministry of the good Samaritan will be the healing work of the Holy Ghost. . .The glory of the Lord will manifest and bring healing, wholeness, recovery to all who are sent to these houses God has marked as the Inns.. (*My first guest was sovereignly healed of a 20- year torn meniscus, and I've been told this will be a house of teaching, healing and peace and glory.*)

"Many think that quantity and numbers mean that it's the blessing of God, but the Lord revealed to me that **it's quality He is after and building real relationships and real discipleship.** (*I've always had smaller groups and even individuals whom I've poured into, and I've been adamant about being real,-speaking the truth in love, confessing and submitting one to another, -etc. as I've discipled many through the years.*)

"As house churches they **will minister face to face and individually too, working with small groups**..so they can be <u>trained</u> <u>and equipped. - The Lord wants this quality time given to the babes and even for the return of the prodical sons..</u>(*The Lord told me to be prepared for the return of the prodigals and keep the party favors ready.*)

"Many apostolic prophetic house churches will be set up and planted in all the regions, cities, and states God has marked for His glory. .and it's male and female...meaning apostolic/prophetic fathers and mothers in the family of God.

"I see apostles traveling, going to different states, cities, regions, to birth or help establish other house churches, because of the harvest coming in. In the house churches like the Inn..are **skilled workers, builders, deliverance ministers, who bring real recovery..** They will be places to recover fully.. with real healing balm...Real healing oil will flow.. even rest and restoration, and it<u>'s going to feel like Home..</u>

"W<u>e **will see the true mothers rise up**</u> as the type of nurturing, hostess with the mostest. (*I've already shared about being a Mom to many, and I have been enjoying cooking for some of them that need that too.*)

"They **will host the Glory of the Lord in the houses God has placed them in..**(*The Lord wakes me up almost every night so that I can worship and pray and keep His presence strong.*)

Glory houses..Apostolic House Churches..---this is a mighty move of God, and these houses will be Holy unto the Lord and be Houses of Prayer..(*He is my life, I cherish every moment I can be before Him, I do not get distracted by the world.*)

Tell the people to **forsake not, the assembling of themselves together,** for you will need to be strengthened by each other, and to walk in love - to show love, and give love." (*Love and Life are what the Lord said I would be pouring out to the Body.*) *end.*

Chapter 9

Conclusion

The Lord has led me in a wilderness path for over 45 years to humble me, to test me, to know what was in my heart, if I would keep His commands or not, so that I would experience His life and His great salvation. He did it so that in the end, it might go well with me as He intended and desired. (see 1Cor 10 and Deut. 8:16).

And through this book, I am sharing the new life (that came out of my death) in the path of God's Ways and how all of God's people can successfully make it through also, because it's not by our own righteousness, our own ability or strength, our own knowledge or works, but by our submission to one another and to those He has put over us, and by our obedience to Do His Commandments, and by our trust in the Lord and the faith of the Son of God.

One prophet said that "the last move of God will be about Purity, Holiness and the Fear of the

<u>Lord.</u>" This really excites me since this is what I've been living and teaching for many years, so I know the great benefit and importance of them in my own life and how necessary they are to the Body of Christ. These virtues have never been of too much interest to most in the Body of Christ before, but they will be, as the Body wakes up to the fact that there will be no LIFE, no lasting Glory without them. Everything God commands us to do is always for our highest benefit and welfare, but we can be slow to learn that. It's like we have to hang on to our own wills until every last drop of strength is gone before we will give it up and let God have His way. We are so foolish to want to do things our own way.

MY Firebrands! - A Word by Dana Jarvis

"This is my Remnant prepared and ready to rule and reign with me. -You can feel the magnetism and power of My Presence even from afar. Within they roar, for I Am deeply abiding within them.

I am now releasing My power, My glory, and My authority through them. They have gone through much abuse and brokenness under the wrath and hypocrisy of men. However they arose from the ashes and I have called them unto Me and have chosen them for such a time as this! They are My FIREBRANDS!

Walking with God is a glorious thing because He is so glorious and because of how everything He does and says is totally in perfect wisdom and perfect love. It is a continual discovery only made known to those who obey Him and trust Him in keeping His

Commandments. I have learned that it is obedience that releases revelation. We have to keep obeying and doing - even though we don't know where we're going - just like Abraham. However God is doing great things in our lives and fulfilling all of His will and His promises as we obey.

I marvel at how perfect God's ways are and how He hIdes his wisdom and love for those who obey and live in the Secret Place. I understand why the word says that the righteous will have a continual feast. God brings such joy to our hearts as we discover His Presence and intent in our keeping his Commandments.

When we walk with pure hearts before Him, he will reveal his purity towards us. We will continually see and experience this in everything we do. We will be those whose Paths grow brighter and brighter unto the perfect day. And we will be those who go from glory to glory and from strength to strength. And nothing will be able to separate us from the love of God that He has for us and His love expressed through us.

The word says to taste and see that the Lord is good. That means we must have His fruit in order to see and taste just how wonderful He is. He has promised that if we we will to do his will then we will know what doctrines are from Him.

We will reap what we have sown whether we like it or not, or whether we know it or not. (The word says my people perish for a lack of knowledge.)

We are called to be devoted to one another in brotherly love. And to honor one another above yourselves. (see 'Romans 12:10') In other words, we shouldn't try to get more out of a relationship than what we are putting into it because if the balance is tilted towards our benefit it is unjust. - but good things happen in a relationship if the balance tilts towards the other's benefit Building a good relationship with someone will mean that you can speak the truth in love when they need it and they will probably trust you and the Body will be built up. We should exist for the fulfillment of His love towards others and not for our own fulfillment.

Susan Vercelli wrote: "We need to flow together as one on the Highway of the Lord, in the direction of the union in His Will. Together on this Higher-way, we become A FORCE TO BE RECKONED WITH THROUGH OUR AGREEMENT and UNION WITH HIM!"

What we sow, we will also reap, but what we reap will not look like the original seed, but we will reap the new form, the fruit, that the seed produced and it will be abundant fruit.

Jesus said He was the seed that had to fall into the ground and die and that His death would bear much fruit. which we know has happened. However, His death did not just reproduce unfathomable multiplied numbers of Believers, but also His very life and essence was given to be reproduced within each one in order to have a mature harvest one day that looked and tasted just like Him.

> *For if while we were enemies we were reconciled to God through the death of His Son, it is much more certain, having been reconciled, that we will be saved [from the consequences of sin] by His life [that is, we will be saved because Christ lives today].* (Romans 5:10, Amplified Bible AMP)

Although I am only one very miniscule part of the crop of fruit produced by Jesus' death, nevertheless, according to His Word and the witness of His Spirit, I know that I am one in whom the seed has reproduced after its kind in me. I don't share this fact to boast of anything about myself, but to share with the Body of Christ that the Lord wants us to be willing to let Him complete His work in us so that He can have His full harvest of many brethren who are just like the Firstfruits.

God had me write this book to share with you what HE DID for me as I just obeyed and trusted Him. Yes, I went through much pain in dying to myself for the first 30+ years of my walk with God, but **Now I Am Alive**! He didn't just restore years to me, or just change my circumstances or give me things to make me happier, He gave me a **BRAND NEW LIFE!!** And this NEW LIFE is blessed, prosperous, full of love, peace and JOY! It is CHRIST IN ME, the hope of Glory. It is a life full of His power and authority so that I've become an overcomer who has been putting all my enemies under my feet, (as the Lord has been delivering them over to me little by little.) It's a life of Victory! We get to walk by His Strength, His Wisdom, His Knowledge, His love!—and it is what He wants to do for each of us.

Let us not be one of those who are unwilling to let God complete His work in our lives and in the earth. He bought our lives with a very costly price so we belong to Him, but will we fully let Him have what He paid for? Every time that God has moved to restore Truth to the Church, some religious believers have always resisted the change and God has moved on without them. We must choose whether we will let God have His way in us or not. It is His will and purpose to perfect that which concerns us, but it will not be forced on us. He purposely set a high price for the gold of our full redemption and we have to pay the price if we want to be fine gold; we have to go through the fire; we have to die to LIVE.

The Lord has called us to live in unity and love, but we don't realize how humanly impossible it is to walk in unity and love because of our old selfish sin nature. Without our full realization, sin negatively affects everything about us in so many ways and in addition our sin leaves the door open to the enemy's attacks and lies, making it even more impossible to come into unity and love.

If every Christian would take up their cross and die to their flesh, we would be remarkably surprised to see how wonderful our lives could be and how good and pleasant it would be for us to live together in unity. His love in us that would replace all the bad fruits of the flesh, takes life into a whole nother realm - above all that we could know or think to ask for.

> *I therefore, a prisoner for the Lord, urge you to walk in a manner worthy of the calling to which you have been called, with all humility and gentleness, with patience, bearing with one another in love, eager to maintain the unity of the Spirit in the bond of peace. There is one body and one Spirit—just as you were called to the one hope that belongs to your call* (Eph 4:1-4, ESV)

> *Rather, speaking the truth in love, we are to grow up in every way into him who is the head, into Christ,*
> *from whom the whole body, joined and held together by every joint with*

which it is equipped, when each part is working properly, makes the body grow so that it builds itself up in love. (Epi 4:15-16)

Therefore be imitators of God, as beloved children. And walk in love, as Christ loved us and gave himself up for us, a fragrant offering and sacrifice to God. (Eph 5:1-2)

New Paradigm:

Because the Lord has told me I would be part of bringing in a new paradigm, this word by Wanda Alger is a real blessing to me. "When this coming **wave of glory comes**, everything will change. Nothing will be the same and we will no longer "judge by the cover." For those who have learned to recognize God's glory and the work of the Holy Spirit, <u>a new paradigm will emerge</u> and <u>kingdom realities will displace old belief systems</u> that <u>no longer</u> <u>bring life</u>. However, for some, the changes will be so outside their comfort zone, they will be unable to "hold it together." The Lord is telling us now so that we can work to preserve the unity of our faith through those things that truly make us one. - It is the unconditional love of the Father, salvation through Jesus Christ, and the indwelling power of the Holy Spirit that reflect and illustrate just Who our God is. We must acknowledge and honor each of these aspects of the Godhead if we are to see the fullness of heaven's glory released. - we purpose to walk and work together, even **through our various perspectives, ideologies, and beliefs**." by Wanda Alger

Final Generation Word By Kathy Mote:

This is His final generation of mature sons and daughters through whose ministries - multitudes will be discipled and raised up to maturity and strength.

Soon Everyone is about to receive a life changing revelation and a paradigm shift—and the **Greatest Wealth in the world will be to learn to Walk in the Spirit!!!**

Even the natural realm is subject to the power of God! Peace and strength, power and deliverance are not of the flesh, they are of the Spirit!"

The Lord told me years ago that I would be imparting LOVE and LIFE to the Body of Christ, and I believe the way of LOVE and walking in the Fruit of the Spirit and not just Gifts of the Spirit is what is coming to the Body now.

As I've been filled more and more with God's love for me, I've been able to walk in more and more love towards God and others.

I have progressively been seeing Him bring His Kingdom love and fruit forth in and through my life, and it is being revealed to me just how God wants us to do everything in Love, just as He loves. And this Love walk has brought new life and freedom to me as it will to all of us.

Many of you are going to birth some of the greatest books and messages ever released because of what you are experiencing in your personal prison

"Those who have submitted themselves to the road of the cross through self-denial are the ones that shall be raised up by God to operate as 1 nation under God."

By Pieter Kirstein, God's End-time Eagles, Excerpt:

"God's end-time gathering of the saints, DURING THE STORM OF TRIBULATION, were prophesied in Isaiah 4 and the 7 women is the church of Jesus Christ spoken to in the 7 letters in the book of Revelation that shall take hold of the One New Man company of forerunner sons and daughters of God, meaning they shall latch unto the end-time ministry of the Holy Spirit that works through these surrendered vessels.

"It's time to release the Melchizedek Priesthood. The people of my PRESENCE of My GLORY of My POWER."

Addendum

<u>**Practical steps we need to take if we want His New Life and to be a part of His Apostolic House Churches:**</u>

- Spend quality time in God's presence and in His Word daily
- Seek His Kingdom and His righteousness FIRST
- Grow to love the Lord with all your heart, soul, strength & love your neighbor as yourself
- Practice living His Word in every situation
- Pray through what you have read or heard to make it your own
- Confess your sins and where you have fallen short
- Receive the Lord's forgiveness which will cause you to grow in
- His love and be with no condemnation remaining

- Forgive everyone who has hurt you and release them
- Bless your enemies and do good to them
- Use the Sword/Word against the enemy where you have problems obeying, believing; decree your victory
- Overcome every hinderance by the Blood of the Lamb, the word of our Testimony, and DO NOT love your life unto death.
- Rejoice always and give thanks for how God will use everything for your good in every situation
- Love His appearing
- Keep Humbling yourself
- Keep believing His promises
- Endure unto the end

"PRAYER: Father we ask for the grace to be Doers of your Word and not readers only. Let this book be an inspiration to me to walk in the Narrow Path. Work in me to Will and to Do your good pleasure that you may be glorified. Thank You that You have promised to perfect that which concerns me and that You will finish the work in me because Your ways are perfect and Your love never fails. Thank you that You've given me your Holy Spirit to bring these things to my rememberance and that You will perfect that which concerns me because You are Faithful who has called me and You will do it! It is Finished! In Jesus' name, Amen

This is Dorothy Lee's first book and it describes the process God took her through for 30 years to teach her His Ways on the Narrow Path so that she could die to herself.

It is recommended reading before reading her new book "Now I'm Allive" if you want to get the fuller picture of God's dealings.

Available through honor355@gmail.com, or through my Web site at www.apostledorothylee.org or through Amazon.com

Soaking CD inspired by the Lord

Printed in the United States
By Bookmasters